This book is sponsored by the Chinese Fund for the Humanities and Social Sciences.

China Executive Leadership Academy Pudong (CELAP), a Shanghai-based national institution, is funded by the central government and supervised by Organization Department of the CPC Central Committee. Our training is for senior leaders from government and top executives from the business community. We focus on social improvement and economic development. CELAP was officially opened on 18 March, 2005.

CHINESE URBAN TRANSFORMATION

A TALE OF SIX CITIES

CHEN YUANZHI, ALAN HUDSON & HE LISHENG

RIBA Publishing

© RIBA Publishing, 2018

Published by RIBA Publishing, 66 Portland Place, London, W1B 1NT

ISBN 978 1 85946 629 2

The rights of Chen Yuanzhi, Alan Hudson & He Lisheng to be identified as the Authors of this Work has been asserted in accordance with the Copyright, Designs and Patents Act 1988 sections 77 and 78.

British Library Cataloguing-in-Publication Data
A catalogue record for this book is available from the British Library.

Commissioning Editor: Alex White
Project Editor: Daniel Culver
Production: Richard Blackburn
Designed and typeset by Full Point Creative Media Ltd
Printed and bound by Page Bros, Norwich, UK
Cover image/Image credits: 699pic.com

While every effort has been made to check the accuracy and quality of the information given in this publication, neither the Author nor the Publisher accept any responsibility for the subsequent use of this information, for any errors or omissions that it may contain, or for any misunderstandings arising from it.

www.ribapublishing.com

CONTENTS

ACKNOWLEDGEMENTS

This book is the product of the Oxford University–CELAP Joint Centre for Urban Studies and is supported by the Chinese Fund for the Humanities and Social Sciences. Associate Professor Chen Yuanzhi, Professor Alan Hudson and Professor He Lisheng were the joint project leaders, working out the book's overall structure and the topic for each chapter.

Team members include:
Deputy General Director Liu Genfa, Professor Zhu Ruibo, Professor Chu Tianjiao, Deputy Director Ding Jinfeng, Austin Williams, Dr Yang Zhiqiang, and Associate Professor Ge Yixiang. The authors of the first drafts of each chapter are as follows:
Preface (Alan Hudson, Chen Yuanzhi)
Chapter 1 (He Lisheng, Chu Tianjiao)
Chapter 2 (Chu Tianjiao)
Chapter 3 (Liu Genfa, Chu Tianjiao)
Chapter 4 (Ding Jinfeng, Chu Tianjiao)
Chapter 5 (Austin Williams)
Chapter 6 (He Lisheng, Chen Yuanzhi, Zhu Ruibo)
Chapter 7 (Alan Hudson, Chen Yuanzhi)
Chapter 8 (Yang Zhiqiang)
Chapter 9 (Zhu Ruibo, Yang Zhiqiang)
Chapter 10 (Chu Tianjiao)
Chapter 11 (Chen Yuanzhi)
Chapter 12 (Chen Yuanzhi)
Conclusion (Chen Yuanzhi, Alan Hudson).

Chen Yuanzhi and Alan Hudson revised the whole book on the basis of the first drafts. They also adapted and improved the translated version of the book. Chen Yuanzhi undertook the task of obtaining the copyright of all the photos used in the book.

The project received substantial help from the following organisations: Shanghai Academy of Social Sciences, Nanchang Organization Department of CPC Committee, Qingdao Organization Department CPC Committee, Hangzhou International City Research Center, Chengdu Organization Department of CPC Committee, and Hefei Municipal Government. These organisations helped to arrange the field study agendas, provided case study materials and contributed their thoughts regarding city development. Thank you to all of them.
The present book has benefited enormously from the hard work and professionalism of our editorial team at RIBA Publishing. In particular, we would like to acknowledge the contributions of our Commissioning Editor, Alex White.

Dr Chen Yuanzhi, Associate Professor at the Department of Academics, CELAP

Alan Hudson, Director of Programmes in Leadership and Public Policy, Oxford University Department for Continuing Education

Dr He Lisheng, Director of the Teaching Affairs Department, CELAP

PREFACE

The scale and the rapidity of urbanisation in China is one of the most astonishing and significant phenomena of our times. As late as 2008 the Chinese government was projecting an urbanisation rate of 50 per cent by 2040 but by the end of 2017 the National Bureau of Statistics of China reported that the rate had already hit 59 per cent.

It is easy to be overwhelmed by the numbers but they tell only the smallest part of the story. Behind the numbers are the scale of economic development, intense discussion and elaborate government policies on the nature of urbanisation, and the shaping of the city environment itself. To trace the path of China's urbanisation is not only important in itself but it has global implications. The size and growth of China affects everyone and the scale and dynamism of urban development in China is the touchstone for the nature of the city in this century.

China combines cutting-edge technology and sophisticated infrastructure on the one hand and an extensive less-developed hinterland on the other. This makes it a potential model for advanced economies and those countries at much earlier stages of industrialisation, urbanisation, and modernisation. China's urban life is the contemporary reality of the earlier concept of uneven and combined development.

Traditional concerns such as urban density, green- and brownfield siting, and the relation of suburbs (periphery) to business and historic centres (core) are all under review and reconfiguration. These questions are of the most immediate interest and the book will be, we hope, of most practical use to the wide range of professionals working in the urban field in all, or any, of its aspects.

The book is organised to lead the reader through the developmental process China has undergone. Chapter 1 records China's urbanisation from the birth of the People's Republic in 1949, and simultaneously records the challenges faced in this period and the emergence of strategies, policies, and responses. Here it becomes clear that Chinese policymakers came to realise that a narrow definition of urbanisation as industrialisation alone was inadequate. By the early years of this century a much more rounded set of goals summarised urban development: economic efficiency, environmental protection, and social justice.

The next section of the book attempts to elucidate the policies designed to implement this complex set of aspirations. Chapter 2 deals with the relationship between the function of the city economically and its spatial configuration. This is a story of the shift from the planned economy to a more open economic framework beginning in 1978. This led to industrial zoning and the shifting of much heavy industry from urban centres.

Chapter 3 examines the ownership of land and property relations, the distinction between urban and rural landholding and its implications for urban growth. It addresses the reforms made to accommodate the scale of economic development and urban growth. An immediate consequence of city growth is the need to upgrade and expand community and social provision. In Chapter 4 we look specifically at community involvement in the governance of cities especially at neighbourhood and street level.

In Chapter 5 Austin Williams investigates the impact of ecological thinking on the Chinese urban environment and specifically at the definition and practices of China's 'eco-cities'.

Chapter 6 marks a transition in the text and has two features. It first reviews the literature that had the most impact on urban thinking in China and which, until recently, set the guidelines for urban practice. Second, it reports, in detail, the results of a major survey undertaken by ourselves, and colleagues at the Chinese Executive Leadership Academy Pudong (CELAP). This establishes an urbanisation index for 289 Chinese cities. The chapter demonstrates the continued importance of quantitative analysis in Chinese urban thinking but also the growing awareness of what we would call issues of 'liveability'.

Each of the chapters (7 to 12) in the final section of the book is a case study of one Chinese city. The factors of historical development, spatial planning, economic priorities, infrastructure, social provision, and cultural heritage are given specific and concrete expression. These chapters give examples of exactly how the framework and priorities of urban development work.

There is no way that any six given cities can be fully representative of the Chinese experience. The six examples are not, however, arbitrary or random. The cities give a range of size, geographical and historical position, economic differentiation, spatial planning, and other circumstances to highlight the most significant trends and priorities identified. The pace of Chinese urban development is a continual challenge to anyone attempting to present the current situation. We hope that this text provides the necessary framework and trajectory of this transformative process and that our readers will better understand the environment in which they may come to work.

THE PROCESS AND ORIENTATION OF CHINA'S URBANISATION

Urbanisation follows inexorably from economic development and successful urbanisation is a prerequisite for both further economic development and social and environmental well-being. China's urbanisation in the period following the foundation of the People's Republic in 1949 was closely associated with the single index of industrial development. China became more urban but relatively slowly and with little diversification in the economy. The pace of urbanisation and a new and broader understanding of what it means to shape a new urban environment have followed from the economic reforms initiated in the late 1970s. In the last few years the shift in policy and urban thinking has gained pace, making China's urban experience crucial not only in terms of quantity – there are many people – but also in quality through urban study and policy implementation.

With a large population of around 1.3 billion, China's urbanisation trajectory will exert tremendous influence not only upon its own development but also on the world. China's urbanisation process is of particular importance because of its speed and scale. It took six decades for China's urbanisation to expand from 10 per cent to 50 per cent. The same process took 150 years in Europe and 210 years in Latin America and the Caribbean (China National Human Development Report, 2013).[1] The US economist Joseph E. Stiglitz pointed out that urbanisation in China and high technology in the United States would be the two crucial arenas to exert influence on development in the 21st century.[2] The urbanisation development path and the experience of urbanisation in China are exemplars especially for the many countries throughout the South with the same opportunities for urban development that have been demonstrated in China. This chapter describes the development process and present state of China's urbanisation. It examines future policies and possibilities for the healthy development of China's urbanisation.

The Development Process and China's Current Urbanisation

Urbanisation here means the shift from an agricultural population to a non-agricultural population and the centralisation of resources for production and livelihood.[3] Since the population of China constitutes one-quarter of the total population of the developing countries in the world, its urbanisation cannot help but be highly influential. Between 1975 and 2000, the urban population of the world increased by 1.317 billion, with a yearly increase of 52.68 million. The urban population of the developing countries increased by 1.164 billion, with a yearly increase of 46.52 million – by far the biggest component of the historic shift to urban life. In China itself from 1978 to 2003, the urban population increased by 351.5 million, with a yearly increase of 14.05 million. This accounted for 26.7 per cent of the global yearly urban population increase, and

30.2 per cent of that in the developing countries. In the near future, the healthy development of China's urbanisation has to contribute to solving a series of China's major strategic problems. In doing so, China's urbanisation will be of historic significance to the world.

The Development Process of China's Urbanisation

Since the founding of the People's Republic of China (PRC) in 1949, China's urbanisation has been a function of the planned economy period and then the market economy period.[4] Figure 1.1 shows China's urbanisation rate from 1949 to 2012.

Emphasis on the Development of Heavy Industries (1952–65)

In the early years of New China, the government implemented a strategy of prioritising the development of heavy industries. Under this strategy, a large amount of rural labour entered state-owned enterprises to work, and industrial cities – particularly the inland industrial cities – had priority and developed quickly. During this period, the proportional increase in the urban

population exceeded that of national population as a whole:

- From 1952 to 1965, the national urban population increased from 71.63 million to 130.45 million, an increase of 82.1 per cent.

- During the same period, the national population increased from 574.82 million to 725.38 million, an increase of 26.2 per cent.

- The percentage of the urban population in the national population increased from 12.5 per cent in 1952 to 16.3 per cent in 1958, and then to 18.0 per cent in 1965.

China's planning has been organised around successive Five-Year Plans since 1953. Large-scale industrialisation turned a large number of peasants into workers. The year-on-year increase in the urban population between 1949 and 1958 was 0.63 per cent. Under the planned economy this rural labour flowed into urban areas through controlled channels such as employment, army enrolment, and university/college enrolment.

From 1958 to 1965, China experienced dramatic fluctuations. From 1958 to the first half of 1960,

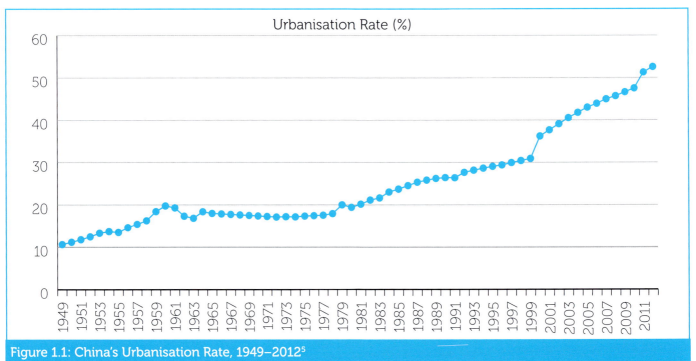

Figure 1.1: China's Urbanisation Rate, 1949–2012[5]

the Chinese government initiated the 'giant leap', described as a socialist development campaign for industry and agriculture. The aim was to drive forward industrialisation using China's abundant labour resources and an atmosphere of revolutionary zeal to enable China to surpass other nations. In this context, 30 million peasants migrated into urban areas and the national urbanisation rate increased by 1.45 per cent each year. The rapid urban shift led to crop failure, a serious shortage in the urban food supply, and famine. Twenty-six million people returned to rural areas between 1963 and 1965 and urbanisation stalled.

'The Cultural Revolution' (1966–77)

From 1966 to 1977, China was in a state of chaos and disorder called the 'Cultural Revolution'. One consequence of this momentous upheaval was the stagnation of any sort of urban development. There was an exodus from the cities. More than 10 million young people as well as millions of government officials and intellectuals moved to rural areas. Although many peasants moved in the opposite direction, the net number of migrants from urban to rural areas was more than 5 million. Meanwhile, the government invested a large amount of capital in the development of industrialisation in inland areas far from traditional urban sites and concentrations of manufacturing. The shift of military and heavy industrial enterprises was primarily a preventative strategy to guard against a feared foreign intervention. The new industrialisation followed the guideline of 'decentralizing large works and aggregating small works'.[6] Factories were located and arranged following the principle of 'being near mountains, scattered and well-hidden'.[7] There was little investment in urban construction, and therefore very few new cities emerged during this period. From 1965 to 1975, the growth rate of the national population exceeded that of the urban population. The percentage of the urban population, 18.0 per cent in 1965, fell to 17.3 in 1975, before creeping up to 17.9 per cent in 1978.

Reform and Opening-up (1978–96)

In 1978 a policy of reform and opening-up was implemented around the concept of a socialist market economy. As a corollary, urbanisation was back on the agenda. Many towns and counties were upgraded into cities. There were 191 cities in 1978 and 666 in 1996. The urban population increased from 17.9 per cent to 29.4 per cent of the total population. In this 18-year period, China's urbanisation rate increased by 11.8 per cent.

1996 Onwards 'Deepening Reform and Expanding Opening-up'

The preceding two-decade period of reform and opening-up brought about economic development, capital investment, and an increase in per capita income. The construction of Development Zones, new districts and the beginnings of the internationalisation of some cities drove the development of China's urbanisation into a new phase. During this period, the tide of economic globalisation enhanced the opening-up of China's economy. China's economic transition also accelerated the progress of marketisation, with stronger market demands for urbanisation. Meanwhile, a series of institutional innovations made by the government not only reduced the transaction cost of urbanisation, but also reduced risks and improved the anticipated gains of urbanisation. China's urbanisation entered an accelerated development phase, with the urbanisation rate rising from 29.4 per cent in 1996 to 52.6 per cent in 2012, an increase of 23.2 per cent. The national urban population increased from 359 million to 710 million.

The Main Characteristics of China's Current Urbanisation

Such a rapid expansion rate for such an extended period is quite rare in the history of urbanisation. The development speed of China's urbanisation has been about twice the world's average development speed of urbanisation. The processes of urbanisation in different countries vary greatly (Figure 1.2). China has been for some time on a fast-moving highway of urbanisation.

The new policies after 1978 encouraged millions of agricultural workers to seek economic opportunity, in city factory work. This was mainly in the developed coastal areas, particularly in the deltas of the Pearl and Yangtze Rivers, as well as the capital Beijing. This was made possible by the loosening of China's household management system, or *hukou*, which still remains in place. By the end of the 1980s there were 30 million migrant rural workers but the number climbed to 226 million by 2012.

On the one hand, the living and housing costs in big cities put a great strain on migrant workers' incomes because their residency qualification made them ineligible for any form of social and welfare provision. On the other, they still held the right to use farmland in their hometowns, as well as to possess housing and reserved land. If they lived single lives, as many of them did, they could still make cash transfers back to their home village. Estimates for 2012 are that only 17 per cent of migrant workers are designated as permanently settled down in cities and therefore a real urban population; 83 per cent of them had still not acquired an urban *hukou*. Nevertheless, despite this anomaly that economic policy encourages internal migration while social provision inhibits it, the economic pull of urban opportunity is the defining feature of China's urbanisation.

The world's urbanisation history shows that generally a country enters the phase of rapid urbanisation when its rate reaches 30 per cent, and that its urbanisation will slow down when the rate reaches 70 per cent.

- In 1978, China's urban population was only 17.9 per cent.

- In 1996, it reached 30.48 per cent.

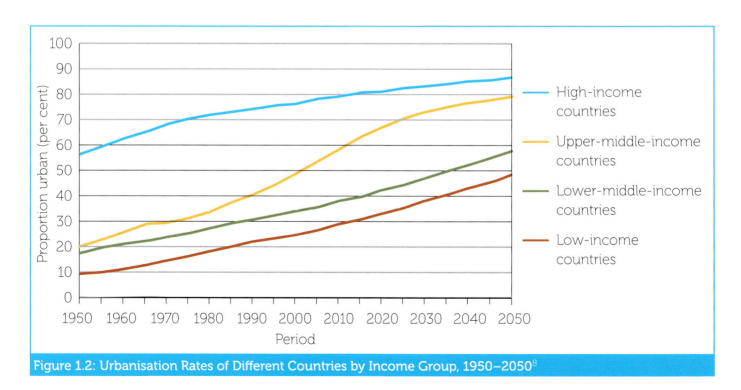

Figure 1.2: Urbanisation Rates of Different Countries by Income Group, 1950–2050[8]

- Between 1996 and 2006, the percentage increased yearly by 1.34 per cent, almost twice the average increase rate between 1978 and 1996.

- By the end of 2012, the percentage had reached 52.6 per cent, a year-on-year increase of 1.54 per cent between 2007 and 2012.

China is still in the period of 'accelerated' urbanisation (see Figure 1.3).

Manufacturing industry (the secondary sector) has always been the backbone of China's economic development, and it is the main urban employer. However, the tertiary or service sector will gain increasing influence in future urbanisation. In 2012, the percentages of the first, second, and third sectors in China's economic structure were respectively 10.1 per cent, 45.3 per cent and 44.6 per cent. As per *China's Flow Population Development Report of 2013*, the statistics provided by the National Health and Family Planning Commission in 2013 show that the employees in the manufacturing industry accounted for 33.3 per cent, 4.1 per cent lower than in 2011.[9] Employment in the tertiary sector was on the up. For example, the employment in wholesale/retail and in

accommodation/catering in 2013 was respectively 20.1 per cent and 11.3 per cent, 2 per cent and 1.4 per cent higher than in 2011. We can predict that China's future urbanisation will be driven mainly by the rise of the tertiary sector associated with an upgrading of the secondary sector.

Government policy is at the heart of urbanisation. For example, it clearly stated that urbanisation was one of the most important means to resolve the 'three rural issues'.[10] The government asserted a strategy to boost urbanisation in the Tenth Five-Year Plan, adjusting policy that restricted the rural population from flowing into cities, and put urbanisation at the centre of the Eleventh Five-Year Plan. It also allowed for market mechanisms in labour movement and employment, commercial estate development, and urban infrastructure construction. All of which accelerated urbanisation.

Due to the differences in natural, social, and economic conditions across the country, China's urbanisation displays distinct regional variation. In 2012, the urbanisation rate in Eastern China, in Central China, and in Western China was 56.4 per cent, 53.4 per cent and 44.9 per cent

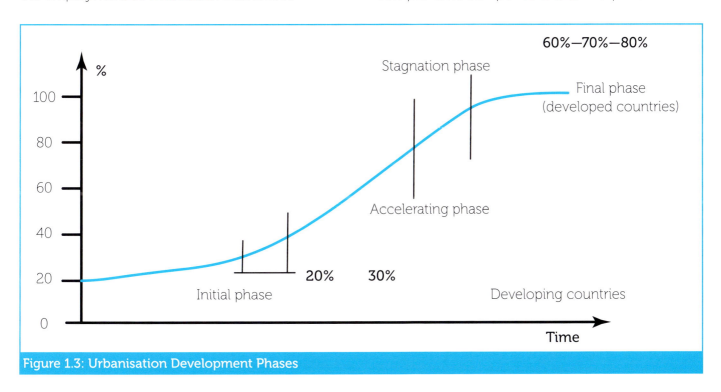

Figure 1.3: Urbanisation Development Phases

respectively. The coastal regions were the first to benefit from opening-up and already had a superior infrastructure that helped to generate a series of city clusters. This development carried over to the inland provinces nearest the eastern seaboard through river, rail, and highway connections. It is only in the last few years in Western China, due to the poorer economic and social conditions and the ecological environment, that urbanisation has taken hold.

Urbanisation and industrialisation, which was achieved in developed countries over more than 200 years, is being completed in China in a matter of decades. This cannot help but produce a whole pattern of interwoven tensions. On the one hand, China's urbanisation has been going forward synchronously with industrialisation; on the other, it has also been confronting challenges from informatisation, marketisation, and economic globalisation. This means that China's urbanisation has occurred as if in a highly compressed and intense time-and-space reactor.

Challenges in China's Urbanisation[11]

Resources and Ecology

Resources (here meaning water, land, and energy) have become a bottleneck in China's urbanisation. In terms of water, China's fresh water per capita is only 1999 m^2, one-quarter of the world average, and this is extremely unevenly distributed.[12] With the dramatic increase in the urban population, the demand for water both for productive and domestic use has soared. Surface water in rivers and lakes and underground water are seriously polluted. Conflicts between urban spatial layout and water resources bearing capacity have become more and more salient. Currently, among 655 cities in China, 400 of them have a shortage of fresh water, and in 200 cities the shortage is serious.[13] The daily shortage of water

for all cities has reached 16 million m^3, and the yearly shortage of water has reached 6 billion m^3, which forces some northern cities to ration water supply.

The shortage of land is severe. The draft summary of the second national land investigation,[14] which started in 2001 and was completed in 2009, reported that the actual area of cultivated land was 2.026 billion mu (Chinese measurement unit)/ 666.5 m^2, closely approaching the 'Red Line' of 1.8 billion mu.[15] China confronts a tough land utilisation problem. On the one hand, the inadequate supply of urban construction land has become the biggest problem in the development of many cities. On the other, there exists much land waste in current urban construction. Of course, historically, cities grow up in areas of high agricultural productivity. The expansion of any given city is therefore potentially at the expense of the best agricultural land.

There is a shortage of energy supply and low efficiency in the existing supply. With the progress of urbanisation, more industry, a higher urban population, and higher per capita domestic consumption there is no end to the demand for more energy production.

Initially, China's urbanisation was almost entirely about industrialisation. Inevitably, this worsened the pollution of solid waste, water, and air and recently traffic pollution added to the problems. Pollution treatment lagged way behind. In many cities, industries and population are highly concentrated, and the great amount of waste in congested areas has reached far beyond the self-purification capability of an urban environment. Urban pollution has trapped urbanisation in a great ecological dilemma.

Relieving Social Conflicts[16]

The Twelfth Five-Year Plan proposed increasing citizens' incomes, increasing domestic demand, and simultaneously strengthening the economy. In the past, domestic spending has been low because Chinese consumers save disposable income rather than spending it because of the potential cost of health, education, pensions, and other measures of social security. By widening and increasing social provision the government hopes to expand the domestic market for consumer goods. Urban citizens now enjoy a large amount of public service provision; however, peasants working in cities still receive inferior provision. The process of urbanisation needs an expanding labour supply which should be matched by the necessary public goods and a social policy for the whole population.

Measures for China's New Urbanisation

Reports from the Eighteenth National People's Congress of the CPC put forward for the first time that New Urbanisation is the carrier for building an all-round, well-off society.[17] It is the key concept in realising the transformation of overall economic development. The policy orientation of New Urbanisation stresses the following characteristics:

- the principle of people first and ecological protection;

- the co-development of industrialisation, informatisation, urbanisation, and agricultural modernisation;

- the need to make cities more liveable for all citizens, alongside the integrated development of rural and urban areas, within a balanced regional environment;

- an intensive, intelligent, environmentally friendly, and low-carbon urbanisation with Chinese characteristics.

The triumvirate of its aims are: environmental protection, economic efficiency, and social justice.

The Managed Migration of the Rural Population to Urban Areas

The migration of the rural population to urban areas is not entirely a market process. Historically, migrant workers gravitated to the major coastal cities in Guangdong, around Shanghai, and, of course, Beijing. These were the prime areas of economic growth and jobs. This economic pull may have been constrained by the registration restrictions of the *hukou* and the almost complete absence of social provision but it did not stop the migratory flow. Any policy reform needs to both redirect the destination of migrant labour and make lives more comfortable.

The government now encourages rural labour to reside in small and medium-sized cities and towns. This encourages the economic development of such cities while increasing the urban population. It involves less movement for the migrant and makes it easier for them to maintain cash flow, therefore providing beneficial consequences for the rural economy through improvement of agricultural productivity.

At the same time, very large cities still need labour but this is more likely to be either in the service sector or in highly specialised employment opportunities.

The Chinese government aims to set up a database of population flow and job demands, which will provide an information guide in accord with priorities for industrialisation, economic development, urbanisation, and national security.

As is often the case in Chinese policy development, reform of the household registration system is being conducted through pilot schemes at city and provincial level, with no definitive policy having yet emerged.

The Reconfiguration of Urban Space

It is necessary to fully develop large cities and strengthen their influences on neighbouring cities. During the initial and middle stages of urbanisation, the expansion and development of big cities contributed significantly to the level of urbanisation as an important prerequisite for a comprehensive urban system. However, the industrial structure not only became outdated but also environmentally weak and socially impoverished. A new pattern sees heavy industry moved away from the city centre, spreading employment opportunities and with improved infrastructure tackling both environmental and social concerns. The biggest conurbanisations become distinct city regions.

Urban development in China is now characterised by such city regions or urban clusters where one or more big cities are surrounded by smaller cities and towns.[18] In 1976, Jean Gottmann, a French geographer, delineated six metropolitan regions as world class, one of which was the Yangtze River Delta.[19] This is a powerful and developing trend both in China and globally. The GDP of the three metropolitan regions in both the USA and Japan account for 65 per cent and 69 per cent respectively of the total of the country. Currently, there are three metropolitan regions in China: Beijing–Tianjin–Hebei, the Yangtze River Delta, and the Pearl River Delta. These regions account for 38 per cent of the total GDP of China.

While these city regions will continue to be hugely important and have a growing global impact, much of China's urban development must be at the scale of small and medium-sized cities and towns developing according to their own intrinsic advantages.

Effective Use and Conservation of Resources for Environmental Protection

- Building a resource-saving and environmentally friendly society is now a strategic priority, for the long term, in China's state policy for modernisation, as follows: by promoting research on energy-saving technology and formulating policy guidance in key areas of construction and transportation.

- A sustainable urban development orientation, treating the urban environment as a 'complex ecological system of society-economy-environment'.[20] Ecological cost factors have to be included in economic analysis and policymaking. The protection of this urban ecological system must be included as one of the criteria for government performance evaluation.

- A change in the mode of production and consumption. The problem of resource waste and environmental pollution cannot be solved solely by advanced technology and infrastructure construction.

- Remaking land use and planning policies to ensure they are compatible with the market economy. For example, for industrial land use, there needs to be a highest and lowest plot ratio. For real estate land use, there needs to be a cost premium for a low plot ratio. It is also necessary to propose guiding principles for the use of underground space.

Strengthening Urban Planning, Construction and Management

- In drawing up urban plans we must consider the capacity of water and land resources, the topography and geological structure, the inherited economic development and cultural ambience, and the existing infrastructure and public service capacity.

- Urban planning has to be integrated with land use planning, to build an effective and consistent overall template.

- The migration of the rural population to urban areas leads to the decline of the population in villages. This should lead to a rise in agricultural productivity and improvements in both per capita GDP and the quality of life, especially if the population circulation is not constrained by an inflexible registration system.

Implementing a Strategy of 'Industry Nurturing Agriculture' and 'City Supporting Village'

The integration of the urban and the rural is essential for sustainable urban development. The Chinese government is determined to adjust the structure of national income distribution and no longer considers agriculture merely as a source of government income. It now:

- increases investment in the infrastructure of villages, including irrigation, water conservancy and road construction;

- guarantees investment in compulsory education, sanitary systems, and charitable networks for disadvantaged groups;

- researches and formulates land use policies that can balance both construction land use and agricultural use;

- forms an integrated employment market to offer more diverse opportunities for rural people.

Endnotes

1   United Nations Development Programme, *China National Human Development Report 2013, Sustainable and Livable Cities: Toward Ecological Civilization*, Beijing: China Translation and Publishing Corporation, June 2013.

2   Joseph E. Stiglitz, 'China second generation reform strategy', *Economic Daily News*, 13 November 1998.

3   Zhou Ganzhi, 'Exploring the urbanization with Chinese characteristics', *International Urban Planning*, 2009, p. 6.

4   Gao Xincai, Zhou Yi, and Xu Jing, 'Reflections on the historical process of China's urbanization', *Academic Exchange*, issue 1, 2010.

5   Relevant data is released by the National Bureau of Statistics of China (http://www.stats.gov.cn/english/).

6   The Third-Front Movement, https://baike.so.com/doc/5880088-6092963.html

7   ibid

8   United Nations Department of Economic and Social Affairs/Population Division, *World Urbanization Prospects: The 2014 Revision*, United Nations, 2014, p. 35.

9   National Population and Family Planning Commission, *China's Flow Population Development Report of 2013*, China Population Publishing House, 1 July 2013.

10 The three rural issues are agriculture, rural development, and peasants.

11 Zhou Weilin, 'China's urbanization: Inborn mechanism and profound challenges', *Urban Development Research*, issue 11, 2012.

12 Data sources: '2014 Statistical Bulletin on China Water Activities' and *China Statistical Yearbook*, 2015.

13 Data sources: News briefing held by the State Council Information Office on 29 March 2010.

14 The Investigation Bulletin on main data results of the second National Land Survey, http://www.mlr.gov.cn/zwgk/zytz/201312/t20131230_1298865.htm (accessed 5 October 2017).

15 The Red Line of 1.8 million mu cultivated land is regarded as the ultimate bottom line of securing Chinese grain supply.

16 Chu Tianjiao and Tan Wenzhu, *Urban Planning and Urban Administration in Rapid Urbanization*, Shanghai: People's Press, 2012.

17 Hu Jintao, 'Firmly march on the path of socialism with Chinese characteristics and strive to complete the building of a moderately prosperous society in all respects', *Report to the Eighteenth National Congress of the Communist Party of China*, http://www.xinhuanet.com/18cpcnc/2012-11/17/c_113711665.htm (accessed 26 April 2018).

18 Li Jingwen, 'Important development trend of China's urbanization: The appearance of city clusters (circles) and their demands for investment', *Innovation*, issue 3, 2008.

19 Jean Gottmann, 'Megalopolitan systems around the world', *Hrvatski geografski glasnik*, Vol. 38, issue 1, 1976, pp. 103–111.

20 Artur Tuziak, *Socio-Economic Aspects of Sustainable Development on Global and Local Level*, 12 July 2010. Available at SSRN: https://ssrn.com/abstract=1638879 or http://dx.doi.org/10.2139/ssrn.1638879 (accessed 26 April 2018).

CHINESE CITIES: FUNCTIONS AND INDUSTRIAL LAYOUT

2

During the era of the planned economy industrial production was synonymous with urbanisation and at the core of city functions. Industries clustered in the central areas of cities, while production-oriented and life-oriented service industries seriously lagged behind. When reform went in the direction of the socialist market economy, Chinese cities shifted focus to the coordination of production and service functions while life-oriented services still fell behind. Differential land rent paved the way for industries such as finance and commerce to occupy the heart of urban centres, while manufacturing industries shifted to the outskirts. This chapter depicts the evolution of urban industrial layouts along with changes to the dominant urban functions. It highlights the construction of Development Zones and new cities – the important spatial carrier of urban industrial development in China.

Major Functions and Industrial Layout of Chinese Cities

The function of a city refers to the role that it plays in regional or national economic development.[1] When cities change from monofunctional small towns to metropolises of multiple functions, their dominant functions also change. Since industrial layout reflects urban functions in terms of space, the changes in dominant functions have led to the adjustment of industrial layout.[2]

Planned Economy Period: Production Oriented

At its foundation, the People's Republic of China was a pre-industrial society, with an agricultural tradition stretching back for millennia. Cities were not, primarily, sites of production, but commodity exchange centres (markets). They were also centres of political and administrative jurisdiction, supported by the military power of the state. They were consumption-based rather than production-based. In 1952, national industrial production only accounted for 17.6 per cent of GDP. The expansion of industrial production was seen as essential in order to improve living standards and to consolidate the regime of the new government. Therefore, China gave priority to industrialisation.

From the 1950s to the 1970s, China's urbanisation was guided by the strategy of restraining large cities while promoting the development of small and medium-sized ones. In addition, most counties were designated to develop five small-sized industries.[3] The output of secondary industry increased continuously and reached 48.5 per cent of GDP in 1980. Due to the emphasis on the production function of cities and particularly on their role as the manufacturing base, heavy industry developed very fast while light industry and service industry lagged behind. There was a serious shortage of urban infrastructure, service facilities, and housing supply. During this period, productivity and the supply capacity of agriculture significantly dropped behind those of industry. Furthermore, the household registration system also hindered the transfer of rural surplus labour to non-agricultural sectors in cities. Industrialisation was not accompanied by urbanisation. From 1949 to 1980, the number of cities rose from 136 to 193, with an average annual increase of 1.84. The proportion of urban non-agricultural population and the total population increased from merely 9.1 per cent and 10.6 per cent to 13.7 per cent and 19.4 per cent respectively.[4]

Reform and Opening-up Period: Equilibrium between Production and Service

From the mid-1980s, China began to establish the leading role of large and medium-sized cities for regional economic development. China started to support the development of enterprises under all forms of ownership, including SMEs (small and medium-sized enterprises) and rural township enterprises. This motivated a large number of surplus rural labourers to transfer to the non-agricultural industrial sector. The number of cities increased from 193 in 1980 to 668 in 1998, an average annual increase of 26.39 per cent. The proportion of urban non-agricultural population and the total population rose from 13.7 per cent and 19.4 per cent to 23.97 per cent and 30.4 per cent respectively. The role of the tertiary sector in economic development became much more significant. In 1980, it accounted for 21.4 per cent of GDP, and by 1998 it was 32.9 per cent.

The transition from production-oriented cities to service and life-oriented cities began in the 1990s.[5] The fact that more than 50 per cent of the total employed now work in the tertiary sector is an important signal. The rapid development of the real estate, finance and insurance, transport, and postal services sectors gradually strengthened the leading role of the tertiary industry. The tertiary sector came to occupy large areas of land in city centres previously allocated for industrial use. The transition also transformed the nature and space of cities.

Development Zones: New Industrial Space

Development Zones have become an important carrier of urban development. Since 1978, the Chinese urban resident population has increased at a rate of ten million annually. Development Zones offered spatial and industrial conditions for the expanding urban population. The shift was characterised as 'retreating from secondary industry while developing tertiary industry in central urban areas'.[6] The Development Zones offered new industrial space on the periphery while central urban areas were reutilised to develop the service sector.

The Main Categories of Development Zones

Economic Development Zones, in a broad sense, include Special Economic Zones, Economic and Technological Development Zones, Bonded Zones (also known as the Free Trade Area), High and New Technology Industry Development Zones, National Tourism Resorts, and National Pilot Areas of Comprehensive Reform.[7]

Economic and Technological Development Zones

Economic and Technological Development Zones (ETDZs) are specially designated in suburban lots. Predominantly newly built, the ETDZ is export-oriented, covering an area of approximately three to five km^2. It is home to processing industry, equipped with warehouses and necessary commerce, service, municipal utilities, and administrative agencies. There are no permanent residents; dormitories are available for management staff. The construction of ETDZs requires infrastructure investment, generally funded by domestic investors, to attract foreign investment projects. The ETDZ has clear geographical boundaries. It is an integral part of urban land, but not defined as part of the 'built-up area' of cities.

Figure 2.1: Dongying Economic and Technological Development Zone[8]

Bonded Zones

Bonded Zones are places isolated from the impact of domestic economic policies. China's Bonded Zones are enclosed with clear boundaries and without local residents, which are regulated by strict quarantine measures. All products are for export. Bonded Zones encourage foreign capital and advanced technology and management systems.

High and New Technology Industry Development Zones

High and New Technology Industry Development Zones are established to encourage high-tech research and application of research findings. In essence, it is a knowledge-intensive and technology-intensive area. High and New Technology Industry Development Zones are designed to promote the commercialisation,

Figure. 2.2: China's First Free Trade Zone (Shanghai Waigaoqiao Free Trade Zone)

Figure 2.3: Zhongguancun Science and Technology Park

Zhongguancun Science and Technology Park

The park dates back to the 'Zhongguancun Electronics Street' in the early 1980s. In May 1988, the State Council approved the establishment of the Beijing New Technology Industrial Development Trial Zone (predecessor of the Zhongguancun Science and Technology Park). Thus, Zhongguancun became the first high-tech park in China. On 13 March 2009, the State Council approved the construction of the Zhongguancun National Demonstration Zone, and planned to build Zhongguancun a S&T innovation centre with a global influence. Later, the Development Plan Outline for Zhongguancun National Demonstration Zone (2011–20) was launched by the State Council on 26 January 2011.

industrialisation, and internationalisation of domestic high-tech achievements and accelerate the penetration and expansion of new technologies.

National Tourism Resorts

National Tourism Resorts are tailored primarily for overseas visitors. Such resorts include: foreign real estate (mainly export-oriented villas, apartments, flats, office buildings, and other real estate projects), tourism and cultural entertainment (holiday villages and playgrounds, gyms, dance halls, bowling, etc.), tourism infrastructure facilities (roads and communication projects), foreign commerce and services (five-star international hotels and supporting facilities, Chinese and western restaurants, grocery stores and chain stores).

A Brief History of Development Zones

Development Zones are an important driving force in the Chinese economy. At the end of 2006, there were 11,568 national and provincial Development Zones, with a total planned area of 76.29 million km². The history of Development Zones in China can be divided into three stages.

Figure 2.4: Taihu National Tourist Resort

Tourist Resort Area of Taihu Lake, Jiangsu

Taihu National Tourist Resort in Suzhou is one of 12 national-level tourist resorts in the country, approved in October 1992 by the State Council. It covers a land area of 173 km² with a lake surface area of 854 km².

It began with the construction of national Economic and Technological Development Zones and the establishment of national High and New Technology Industry Development Zones.[9] China decided to open up Dalian, Tianjin, Guangzhou, and 14 other coastal port cities in 1984. It also approved the construction of 11 Economic and Technological Development Zones: Dalian, Qinhuangdao, Ningbo, Qingdao, Yantai, Zhanjiang, Guangzhou, Tianjin, Nantong, Lianyungang, and Fuzhou. The purpose was 'to introduce advanced technology needed in China, to develop joint ventures, Chinese-foreign cooperative enterprises, foreign-owned enterprises and Sino-foreign cooperative research institutions, to increase foreign exchange income, to provide new materials and key components, and to absorb new expertise, new technology and scientific management experience.'[10]

This was followed up in 1986 when the State Council approved the establishment of Shanghai Hongqiao and Minhang Economic and Technological Development Zones. These state-level ETDZs played an important role in promoting industrialisation and urbanisation in China.

In order to promote technological innovation and apply scientific and technological research to industry, Zhongguancun Science Park, the first national High and New Technology Industry Development Zone, was set up in Beijing in 1988. During this period, the economy developed rapidly alongside the development of different types of Development Zone. The construction of Development Zones expanded from coastal cities to those along rivers, from eastern provinces to central and western areas in China. The country was 'in a rush for Development Zones'.[11] Over 700 Development Zones had been approved and constructed by the end of 1994. They included 32 national ETDZs, 52 national High and New Technology Industry Development Zones, 13 bonded zones, 11 national resorts, and China–Singapore Suzhou Industrial Park (SIP). All of the bonded zones and 91.7 per cent of the national tourist resorts were still located in the eastern coastal areas.

There are three main features of Development Zones in this period. First, the quantity and quality of foreign capital greatly improved. Multinational companies began to replace SMEs as investors. Technology-intensive projects and foreign R&D centres successively flowed in. Second, unprecedented achievements were made in industrial production, tax revenue, and economic benefits. In 1994, the industrial production in 14 coastal ETDZs rose by 858.2 per cent compared with that in 1991. Third, the economic output of Development Zones accounted for a growing percentage in their host cities. For example, industrial production in the Guangzhou Development Zone accounted for 11.2 per cent of the city in 1996. Development Zones have become the driving forces for the urban economy.[12]

After the 1997 Asian financial crisis, foreign investment in China's Development Zones plummeted. Policymakers were alert to the risks of a one-sided export-oriented economy, especially in Development Zones. During this period, the guidelines for Development Zones changed. Previously, the priority was simply attracting foreign capital. It shifted to attracting both foreign and domestic investment, fostering sustainable development, and promoting industrial restructuring and upgrading.

Many problems, such as poor economic performance and the waste of land resources, were exposed. Since 2004 many zones have merged and reorganised. By 2007, 1,568 national and provincial Development Zones were approved, 223 of which were national Development Zones (Tables 2.1 and 2.2).

Since 2000, Development Zones in China have enjoyed steady growth. During the Eleventh Five-year period, the number of state-level Development Zones increased to 116, their regional production output growing at an average annual rate of 23 per cent and accounting for 7 per cent of the country's total GDP. Their proportion of industrial added value reached 12 per cent and their share of total exports accounted for 16 per cent and tax revenue accounted for 6 per cent. National Development Zones were the driving force for local economic development, accounting for more than 13 per cent of the GDP of the host cities.

The Impact of Development Zones on Urban Industrial Restructuring

Development Zones were established to attract foreign investment and develop High and New Technology Industry and export processing industry. Through the construction of Development Zones, many Chinese cities became more concentrated both in terms of industry and population in a relatively short time. Development Zones also play a significant role in promoting industrial upgrading, optimising urban spatial organisation and improving urban functions.

The interaction between Development Zones and their host cities has gone through two main phases. Mostly located in suburbs, Development Zones were separated from their host cities in the form of 'isolated islands', keeping a certain distance from the city and having clear geographical boundaries in the form of roads and rivers. During this period, the main function of Chinese Development Zones was similar to

Table 2.1: Types and Number of Development Zones in China (2007)

Level	Type	Number	Note
National Development Zones	Total	223	
	Economic and Technological Development Zone	54	Zones entitled with policies enjoyed by national Economic and Technological Development Zones are included, namely Suzhou Industrial Park, Shanghai Jinqiao Export Processing Zone, Ningbo Daxie Economic and Technological Development Zone, Xiamen Haicang Taiwanese Investment Zone, and Hainan Yangpu Development Zone
	High and New Technology Industry Development Zone	54	
	Export Processing Zone	57	
	Bonded Zone	16	
	Bonded Logistics Zone	6	
	Taiwanese Investment Zone	4	
	Cross-Taiwan Strait Technology Industrial Park	2	
	Border Economic Cooperation Zone	14	
	Border Trade Zone	2	
	National Tourism Resort	12	
	Cross-border Industrial Zone	1	ZhuAo (Zhuhai, and Macao) Cross-border Industrial Zone
	Finance Trade Zone	1	Shanghai Pudong Lujiazui Finance Trade Zone
Provincial Development Zone	Total	1,345	
	Economic Development Zone	810	
	Industrial Park	535	Among them, there are 64 High and New Technology Industry parks
Total		1,568	

Source: Compiled based on data issued by the National Development and Reform Commission (NDRC)

Table 2.2: Main Economic Indicators of the National Economic and Technological Industry Development Zone (2014)

Indicator	GDP (CNY, billion)	Industrial Added Value (CNY, billion)	Tax Revenue (CNY, billion)	Total Import and Export (CNY, billion)	Total Export (CNY, billion)	Total Import (CNY, billion)	Actual Foreign Investment (CNY, billion)
Development Zones	7654.5	5569.4	1249.7	5085.8	2791.3	2294.5	385.4
Proportion of Total Country	12%	20.5%	10.5%	19.2%	n/a	n/a	52.3%

Source: Ministry of Commerce

Export Processing Zones. The connection between Development Zones and host cities was weak because raw materials and markets were not localised.

The number and the size of Development Zones increased rapidly in the mid-1990s. Almost all cities had Development Zones and some cities even had more than one. Since 1998, the focus of Development Zones has shifted from attracting foreign investment to attracting domestic investment too. Economic ties between Development Zones and host cities began to be strengthened, in the following ways:

- Development Zones promote the spatial reconstruction of urban manufacturing industry. They aggregate the most competitive manufacturing industries.

- They promote the suburbanisation of the urban population. Affluent communities are gradually formed in Development Zones.

- They occupy a large amount of industrial land. The expansion of industrial land is a dominant factor in China's urban development at this stage. Therefore, the expansion of Development Zones leads to the reconstruction of urban space.[13]

With the concentration of industries, population, and production factors, as well as the continuous improvement of industrial structures and urban functions, the visible and invisible 'boundaries' between Development Zones and other areas of host cities became blurred.

New Towns: Spatial Restructuring of Urban Industries

New towns in China can be traced back to the construction of satellite towns in the 1950s. For the purpose of developing industrial space, some large enterprises were located in the suburbs of metropolitan cities, such as Beijing, Shanghai, and Shenyang, as industrial satellite towns. Factory districts, residential areas, and public service facilities were built in these towns. In general, the supporting facilities were insufficient and were not desirable enough to attract residents. At the end of the 20th century, the development of China's economy, society, and urbanisation showed a sustained and rapid momentum. However, excessive concentration of population and economic and social activities in large cities placed tremendous pressure on city operation. Thus, to develop new urban space, to optimise urban structures, and to enhance the overall

Figure 2.5: Zhujiang New Town, Guangzhou[14]

Chinese Urban Transformation: A Tale of Six Cities

competitiveness of cities became a key issue in the development of major cities. Some cities began to build 'new towns' to expand urban space in an effort to make a more reasonable distribution of industries and population. On the one hand, population in downtown areas could be dispersed, easing the pressure of population and industrial agglomeration. On the other, the government could motivate development of suburban areas.

Li Guiwen et al. (2011) summarised the causes of new town construction.[15] First, agglomeration and diffusion are two complementary paths of urban development. Due to the limitation of resources and space, the existing urban space cannot accommodate all the newly added population. Consequently, urban functions have to be extended to the outskirts, which always leads to the birth of new towns affiliated to old cities.

Second, reform of land policies has changed the spatial layout of cities. Coupled with the development of the real estate market, price mechanisms help to improve the efficiency of land use. So, the central area of the city performs commercial, trade, and financial functions, while industrial, warehousing, and other functions are relocated to the outskirts. New towns in the suburbs of metropolises contribute to realising this transition.

Third, the reform of the urban housing system makes it possible for residents to choose where they live. In the second half of 1998, China terminated the old policy of housing distribution and initiated the new policy of housing purchase. On the one hand, the new policy brought about a boom in the real estate industry. On the other, housing commercialisation put an end to the previous practice of allocating houses as welfare through one's work unit. Previously urban residents lived in workplace-centred settlements. Now, they live in stratum-oriented settlements, thus forming a new residential spatial layout.

Fourth, improved transportation infrastructure shortens the round-trip time between new towns and downtown areas. The development of urban rail transits and rapid bus systems connects the centre with the outskirts.

Endnotes

1. Yu Hongjun and Ning Yue Min, *Introduction to City Geography*, Anhui: Anhui Science and Technology Press, 1983.

2. Chu Tianjiao, 'Evolution in the transformation of city CBD in Singapore and its enlightenment', *Modern City Research*, October, 2011.

3. Five small-sized industries: In the 1960s, this referred to the small iron and steel plants, small coal mines, small power plants, small chemical fertiliser plants, small machinery factories, and later included small cement plants, etc. In 1970, in the fourth Five-year Plan, the central government required that each province and administrative district developed small coal mines, small iron and steel plants, small chemical fertiliser plants, small cement plants, and small machinery factories. And the central government decided to allocate special funds of CNY80 billion for the development of local five small industries. The development of the five small industries changed the structure of China's industrial economy, expanding the proportion of SMEs. But the five small industries also brought about some adverse consequences.

4. Zhou Yixing, *City Geography*, Beijing: Commercial Press, 1997.

5. Research group of China urban planning and the development trend, China Academy of Urban Planning and Design. the 1997–1998 Chinese city planning and development trend, 'Urban Planning Forum Collection', 1998, pp. 3–11.

6. State Planning Commission, *Views on the Measures to Accelerate the Development of Service Industry During the Tenth Five-year Plan Period*, 3 December 2001, http://www.gov.cn/gongbao/content/2002/content_61850.htm (accessed 26 April 2018).

7. Gu Zhaolin and Wang Hesheng, 'The construction and development of China Development Zone' in *China's Urban Development of 30 Years*, eds Niu Fengrui, Pan Jiahua, and Liu Zhiyan, Beijing: Social Science Literature Press, 2009.

8. Dongying Economic and Technological Development Zone is located in Dongying City, Shandong Province. It was founded in 1992 and was approved to be a National Development Zone in 2010.

9. Gu Zhaoli and Wang Hesheng, 'The construction and development of China Development Zone' in *China's Urban Development of 30 Years*, eds Niu Fengrui, Pan Jiahua, and Liu Zhiyan, Beijing: Social Science Literature Press, 2009.

10. Circular of the State Council approved the 'Summary of the symposium on coastal cities', 4 May 1984.

11. Yang Jirui. Theoretical thinking and policy research of the problem of Development Zone[J]. Social Science Research, 1994 (2): 13–17.

12. Wang Fengyu and Zhu Xiaojuan, 'Review and strategic thinking of China Development Zone', *Yunnan Geographic Environment Research*, April, 2006, p. 96.

13. Zheng Guo, 'The development of China's Development Zone and urban space reconstruction: significance and process', *Modern Urban Research*, May, 2011, pp. 20–24.

14. Zhujiang New Town is the economic core of Guangzhou's headquarters economy. In the centre of the town there is a spacious square surrounded by a number of buildings regarded as landmarks, such as Guangzhou TV Tower, the West Tower, the Guangdong Provincial Museum, the City Library, and Guangzhou Grand Opera House.

15. Li Guiwen, Zhang Xueyong, and Zeng Yu, 'Study on the conditions of the construction of new towns in China – taking Beijing, Shanghai, Guangzhou three cities as examples', *Central China Architecture*, February, 2011.

THE LAND PROPERTY RIGHTS SYSTEM AND LAND ADMINISTRATION

3

The Land Property Rights System[1]

China's land system is different from that of most other nations in the world. Land property rights are subdivided into the right to use, the right to earnings, and the right of disposal. The Law of Land Administration of the People's Republic of China stipulates that:[2]

the People's Republic of China implements a socialist public ownership of land, i.e. the ownership by all people and the collective ownership by working people

and that:

urban land shall be owned by all people (i.e. by the country) and rural and suburban land, except otherwise legally designated to the country, shall be collectively owned, including land for building houses, land and hills allowed to be retained by peasants.

After the founding of the People's Republic of China (PRC), urban land ownership changed from private ownership to state ownership. However, urban land accounted for a very small proportion of the national territorial area. It had been owned by the bureaucratic bourgeoisie, feudal landlords, native industrialists and businessmen, self-employed workers, and non-nationals. In the early days of the PRC city governments took over batches of urban land possessed by the

Kuomintang government and confiscated a large number of urban properties occupied by foreign powers and the indigenous bourgeoisie. Land remained in the ownership of native industrialists and businessmen and self-employed workers.

State-owned land and private land coexisted in cities. Until 1955, urban private land could be sold, leased, pawned, and exchanged. On 18 January 1956, the Secretariat of the CPC Central Committee issued Suggestions on the Current Situation of Urban Private Housing Property and the Socialist Transformations, which stipulated that 'all private ownership of urban open space, street premises and other real estate should be returned to the State through appropriate means.' And the use of state-owned urban land 'shall be allocated by the local government without compensation and no rent need be paid'.[3] This was the nationalisation of urban land, so the urban land use system was characterised by no compensation, indefinite duration, and no liquidity.[4]

When China entered a period of reform and opening-up in 1978 it became necessary to rethink the urban land system. The Regulations of the PRC on Chinese–Foreign Equity Joint Ventures issued by the State Council in 1979 stated that:

the investment contributed by a Chinese partner may include the rights to use the land provided for the equity joint venture during the period of its operation. If the rights to use the land have not been considered as part of the investment from the Chinese party, the joint venture shall pay the Chinese Government a fee for land use.[5]

These regulations and policies changed the rules of using urban land without compensation. They were a prelude to the reform of the urban land use system. Shenzhen began to impose land use fees in 1982. By 1988, more than 100 cities levied such fees.

The Provisional Regulations of the People's Republic of China on Land Use Taxation in Cities and Towns was issued by the State Council on 7 September 1988. It stated that land use tax would be collected in cities and towns from 1 November 1988. Taxes on domestic land users would be collected by central government, and those on foreign-invested and foreign enterprises in China would be collected by local governments. The practice of collecting land use fees put an end to the non-compensation land use system, providing valuable experience for

further reform. Shenzhen took the lead in exploring such reform by separating the ownership of land from land use rights.

Under the premise that urban land is state-owned, the local government sold urban land use rights by public bidding and tendering. There were three relevant cases that sold the use rights of state-owned land respectively by agreement, public tendering, and public auction on 9 September, 29 September, and 1 December 1987 in Shenzhen. Just prior to this last case, in November 1987, Shenzhen, Shanghai, Tianjin, Guangzhou, Xiamen, and Fuzhou had all been approved by the State Council as pilot areas for land use reform.

The National People's Congress modified the Constitution in April 1988. The original provisions on 'forbidding land transfer' were amended to 'land use rights can be transferred in accordance with law'. Subsequently, the Land Administration Law also made appropriate amendments to provide a legal basis for the transaction of state-owned land use rights.

Figure 3.1: Simulation of the First Auction on Land Use Rights in Shenzhen

Chinese Urban Transformation: A Tale of Six Cities

The State Council issued the Provisional Regulations of the People's Republic of China on the Assignment and Transfer of the Rights to Use State-owned Land in Urban Areas in May 1990, in which provisions for the assignment, transfer, lease, mortgage, and termination of the rights to use state-owned land were defined. In 1994, the Administration Law of Urban Real Estate was issued, clearly stipulating that 'the State shall practise a compensatory and terminable system for the use of state-owned land in accordance with the law'. Then the 1998 Land Administration Law came into force, making it clear that land use rights could be transferred. All these laws constitute the essential institutional framework of the Chinese land property rights system.

The Administration System for Land Utilisation

Cultivated Land Protection System

Protecting cultivated land is the primary task of land use administration. The CPC Central Committee and the State Council issued Views on Strengthening Land Administration and Prohibiting Unauthorised Occupation of Cultivated Land on 3 March 1986, which for the first time clearly stated the basic national policy to 'cherish and rationally use land, and make practical efforts to protect cultivated land'.[6] Regulations on the Protection of Basic Farmland was promulgated by the State Council in August 1994, stating that farmland protection was included in the legal system. The Land Administration Law was revised in 1999, emphasising two rules: to reclaim the equivalent amount of land should cultivated land be used for other purposes, and to strictly control the use of cultivated land.

Figure 3.2: Relevant Certification for the Right to Use Stated-owned Land

The control system of land use is the core of the land management system. Land is divided into three basic categories: agricultural land, construction land, and unutilised land.[7] The central government establishes a general plan on land use. The dynamic balance between occupying and reclaiming cultivated land is an important measure to ensure that the total amount of cultivated land shall not be reduced. Those who occupy the land for non-agricultural construction should be responsible for reclaiming the same amount of cultivated land of the same quality. Provincial governments are responsible for maintaining the dynamic balance of the total amount of cultivated land within provincial areas.

The Land Use Planning System

The Land Administration Law issued in June 1986 stipulated that the 'governments at all levels shall organise related departments to compile general plans for land use'. Based on the Land Administration Law, China formulated three ten-year national plans for land use covering the periods up to 2000, 2010, and 2020. It is a five-tier land use planning system comprising national, provincial, municipal, county, and township level. The aim is to achieve optimal allocation of land use. The overall system includes a basic agricultural land protection plan, a land consolidation plan, a land remediation plan, a land development plan, and a reclamation plan.

The Administration System for Construction Land

Ways to obtain construction land include: expropriation of rural collective-owned land, allocation of state-owned land in accordance with law, plus measures for transfer and compensation.

Trading System for Construction Land Quotas in Chengdu[8]

In order to coordinate the development between urban and rural areas, Chengdu and some other cities have explored the improvement of the rural land transaction system. This allows for reallocating construction quotas between urban and rural areas. The construction land quota refers to rural collective-owned construction land, including rural housing and ancillary facilities.

Under the supervision of land management departments, the aim is to consolidate landholdings and improve land economy without changing the overall proportions of land allocation. The basic principle is to keep in line with the premise of land use planning, land consolidation planning, urban and rural construction planning, and industrial distribution planning, and to insist on 'not increasing the total amount of construction land and not decreasing agricultural land'. Land quality shall not be sacrificed and peasants' interests shall be respected. Through the implementation of comprehensive consolidation of construction land, the government can turn the original scattered collective-owned construction land into reclaimed farmland and carry out plans to acquire a certain number of collective-owned construction land quotas. This is because the original collective-owned construction land area is larger than the concentrated residential area. And these new collective-owned construction land quotas can be used for urban construction in accordance with the policy of 'increasing the urban construction land quotas while decreasing the rural construction quotas, and keeping the total construction land unchanged'.

Land Management in Development Zones

With the aim of economic development, China has formed the unique Development Zones policy in order to increase allocation efficiency of industrial land. But many problems have been exposed in the process of attracting foreign investment. Land was sold at low prices or given away, which in turn led to a large number of low-value projects. In 1994, the Ministry of Land and Resource and the State Economic and Trade Commission issued a Directory of Projects with Restricted Land Supply and a Directory of Projects with Prohibited Land Supply to resolve these problems. The Ministry of Land and Resource rectified some Development Zones in 2003. The State Council issued the Decision on Deepening the Reform and Implementing Strict Land Administration in October 2004, stressing that industrial land administration should gradually introduce market mechanisms such as bid invitation, auction, and quotation.

The Administration System for the Urban Land Market

The Current Urban Land Market[9]

There are two kinds of land market: the land use rights leasehold market and the land use rights transfer market.

Land Use Rights Leasehold Market

The land use rights leasehold market refers to the market whereby governments assign land use rights to enterprises, institutions, or individuals, by agreement, tendering, or auction. What is assigned by government is not ownership but the right to use the land within a specified period. It is the right to use the ground, not including underground natural resources, minerals, buried treasure, or hidden property. If the authorisation period expires, the land use rights and above-ground buildings are returned to the state.

There are two types of transaction in the land leasing market. The first type is a long-term lease. The statutory maximum authorisation periods for the various types of land in China are: residential land, 70 years; industrial land, 50 years; land for education, science, culture, health, and sports, 50 years; land for commerce, tourism, and recreation, 40 years; integrated function land or other land, 50 years. The other type is short-term lease, from one to ten years. A land leasing agreement should be in accordance with the existing land use planning.

Land Use Rights Transfer Market

The land use rights transfer market refers to the market whereby land use rights can be transferred between land users. The original land user can transfer the use rights again within the authorised period. To be a legal transaction, the process must be under the supervision of the appropriate land administration department. The new land user takes the rights and obligations from the original user after the deal.

Regulations for the Urban Land Market

Basic Methods

On the macro level, the Chinese government regulates the land market by means of industrial, fiscal, credit, and tax policies, and through planning and programming. On the micro level, the government takes measures to maintain fair trade and equal competition in the land market.

The Regulation of Supply and Demand in the Land Market

Land use planning, especially the annual plan, is an effective measure to control land supply. The Central Bank directly or indirectly intervenes to measure and stipulate the quality and quantity of land credit business. The state can affect money supply and demand through financial leverage, rent and tax levels, interest rates and loan-to-value ratio, thus regulating the supply and demand in the land market.

Regulation Innovation: The Land Reserve System[10]

The Land Reserve System is a regulatory innovation through which local governments use market mechanisms to reserve land. There are three main procedures:

- **Land Acquisition.** Authorised by the municipal government, the reserve agencies shall operate in accordance with land reserve plans. The procedures include acquisition application, ownership verification, consultation, cost estimate, programme approval, acquisition compensation, ownership change, and delivery of the land.

- **Land Reserve.** The land reserve agencies are responsible for completing the pre-development of the reserved land before it is assigned to new land users.

- **Land Supply.** Based on urban development planning, land reserve agencies formulate land supply plans. Reserved land can be supplied through bidding, auction, and agreement assignment.

In 1996, Shanghai set up the first land reserve agency (Land Development Centre) in China. Soon after, Hangzhou, Xiamen, Nanjing, Qingdao, Guangzhou, Zhengzhou, and other cities established their own land reserve agencies.

Endnotes

1 Liao Yonglin et al., 'Land market reform: Retrospect and prospect', *China Land*, issue 12, 2008.

2 The Law of Land Administration of the People's Republic of China, http://www.gov.cn/banshi/2005-05/26/content_989.htm (accessed 26 April 2018).

3 Quoted in Bi Baode, *Study on Chinese Estate Market*, Renmin: Renmin University of China Press, 1994, p. 27.

4 Dong Liming, 'The review and prospect of the paid use of urban land in China, *Yunnan Geographic Environment Research*, December, 1992, pp. 16–29.

5 Ministry of Commerce, *The Regulations of the PRC on Chinese–Foreign Equity Joint Ventures*, https://baike.so.com/doc/6703915-6917879.html (accessed 26 April 2018).

6 *Views on Strengthening Land Administration and Prohibiting Unauthorized Occupation of Cultivated Land*, http://china.findlaw.cn/fagui/p_1/290741.html (accessed 26 April 2018).

7 Cultivated land is a kind of agricultural land.

8 W. Xie, Y. Zhang, and Z. Zhang, 'Land ticket mode and its policy change in Chengdu', *Scientific and Technological Management of Land and Resources*, Vol. 3, issue 19, 2013.

9 Chu Tianjiao, 'Land transfer models and standardization research', *Shanghai Economic Forum*, issue 4, 2002.

10 He Fang, 'Development and innovation of land system with Chinese characteristics', *Shanghai Land & Resources*, issue 3, 2012.

COMMUNITY GOVERNANCE IN CHINA

4

The Evolution of the Urban Community Administration System

Street and Residence Administration System in the Context of the Planned Economy

The Emergence of the Street and Residence Administration System in the Context of the Planned Economy

After the founding of the PRC, the Communist Party of China quickly established an urban social administration system. The vast majority of urban residents were organised by their work units. The remaining residents were under the administration of Street Offices and Residents' Committees (referred to as 'RC'). These Residents' Committees evolved from the 'Office of the Takeover Committee'. Peng Zhen, the Mayor of Beijing, submitted a Report on Organizational and Funding Issues of Urban Street Offices and Residents' Committee in 1953, suggesting: 'Residents' Committees must be established as self-governing organisations. Street offices-agents were responsible for organising residents who are not employed by factories, enterprises, state institutions and schools.'[1] The report was approved by the Central Committee of the CPC. The Standing Committee of NPC promulgated the Organization Regulations of Urban Street Offices and Organization Regulations of Urban Residents' Committees in 1954, specifying the concepts, including the nature, status, roles, responsibilities, organisational structure, and relationships with relevant departments and funding sources.[2,3]

The Functional Transformation of the Street and Residence Administration System in the Context of the Planned Economy

Prior to 1954 Street Offices had limited jurisdiction with simple tasks. From then the regulation specified three tasks for Street Offices, transforming their function:

- to handle residents' affairs assigned by the city or municipal district government;

- to guide the work of Residents' Committees, and to collect the views and needs of residents;

- to also deal with household registration, conflict mediation, social relief, urban sanitation, and public health.

In effect, the Street Offices played a supplementary role in the social administration system. Since the 1990s, the role of Urban Street Offices has been greatly enhanced. Currently, the responsibilities of Street Offices cover at least ten aspects:

- economic development;

- urban administration, including sanitation and municipal facilities;

- civil affairs including social welfare, special care and social relief;

- community service, including for the elderly and the disabled and convenience services for residents;

- population administration, including family planning, employment, and floating population administration;

- comprehensive management of the social security provision;

- socialist spiritual civilisation, which includes community culture, community education, community sports, and health care;

- specific tasks assigned by a superior department;

- instructions for the work of Residents' Committees;

- management of CPC membership on a neighbourhood basis.

In 1954, regulations defined the responsibilities of Residents' Committees as follows:

- the public welfare of residents;

- conveying residents' opinions and demands to the local government;

- mobilising residents to be in line with the law and the government's suggestions;

- assisting national police in maintaining public order, and mediating disputes among residents.

The functions of Residents' Committees were expanded in 1989, through the Organizational Law of Urban Residents' Committees. The new responsibilities of Residents' Committees included:

- explaining to the public the Constitution, laws, regulations, and national policies;

- safeguarding the legitimate rights and interests of residents;

- educating people to fulfil their statutory obligations;

- protecting public property, and promoting the spirit of socialism;

- carrying out social service for local residents;

- mediating civil disputes;

- assisting the police in maintaining public order;

- assisting the government with affairs of public health, family planning, social relief, and juvenile education;

- conveying residents' views, requirements and advice to the government or its agencies.

The Main Features of the Street and Residence System in the Context of the Planned Economy

Supervised by the government, the Organizational Regulations of the Urban Street Offices was promulgated in 1954. It specified 'the chairman, vice-chairman and members of Street Offices shall be appointed by municipal districts or a municipal People's Committee of a city'. The chairman and vice-chairman of Residents' Committees were appointed by the Street Office in charge. The higher-level governments exerted control over Street Offices and Residents' Committees by personnel management and financial sponsorship.

After the mid-1950s, most Chinese people were employed by all kinds of stated-owned units, and these units took the responsibility of managing the staff. Street Offices and Residents' Committees were responsible for those who were not employed by these units. Therefore, the Street and Residence Administration System can be regarded as supplementary to the state-owned unit system. Most people who were not employed were old, sick, or housewives. Residents' Committees were set up to maintain public order, to clean, and to resolve conflicts. It was the basic form of urban administration that played an important role in maintaining public order, mobilising residents, and developing convenient services in the context of the planned economy.

The Community Administration System in the Context of the Market Economy

The Emergence of the Community Administration System in the Context of the Market Economy

Along with the transition to a market economy, the social structure in which most people were employed by state-owned units changed. Those who used to be 'unit people' now become 'social people', or 'community people'. A lot of social service functions were detached from the state-owned enterprises and government departments. In the early 1990s, based on the international practice of 'community development', a number of cities were chosen as the pilot cities in community building.

In December 2000, the Ministry of Civil Affairs issued *View on the Construction of Urban Communities Nationwide*, which defined the community as 'a social organic entity formed by the inhabitants living in a certain geographical area', and it stated that 'the community was under the supervision of Residents' Committee'.[4] The CPC Central Committee passed a resolution on Major Issues of Building a Socialist Harmonious Society in 2006. It pledged to 'turn the urban and rural neighbourhoods into communities that are well managed, characterised by civility and harmony'.[5]

The Basic Structure of the Chinese Urban Community Administration System in the Context of the Market Economy

By the end of 2000, according to *View on the Construction of Urban Communities Nationwide*, governments at all levels were urged to form an overall framework to promote community building. The Civil Affairs Department would take the lead with Residents' Committees as organisers, with a brief to encourage the participation of the general public.[6]

At the national level, the Common People Rights Department of the Ministry of Civil Affairs directs from the macro point of view. At the local government level, there is a Steering Committee for Community Building (SCCB) established by the District Committee of the CPC and district government. Two principal leaders from each of the District Committee of the CPC, district government, the district People's Congress, and the Chinese People's Political Consultative Conference (CPPCC) are appointed as director and deputy director of the Steering Committee. The executive officers from relevant departments constitute the membership of the SCCB. The Community Building Office of the SCCB is co-located with the Civil Affairs Bureau, which is responsible for coordinating with relevant departments (see Figure 4.1).[7]

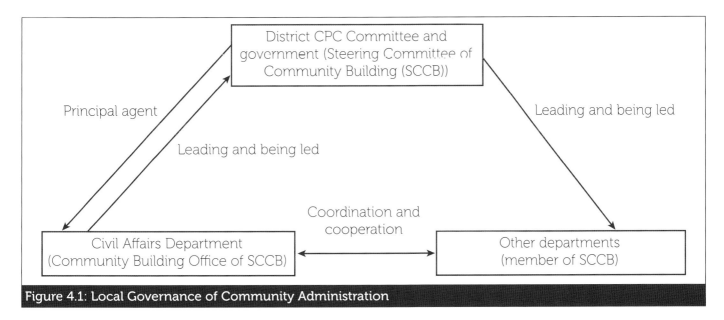

Figure 4.1: Local Governance of Community Administration

Hefei City, in Anhui Province, applied a grid management method to bring together people, places, events, organisations and ideas in a flat structure of community management. By the end of 2011, the method was widely used in the whole city.

In Hefei, there are more than 6,000 grids. Each grid covers an average of 333 households. Each grid has an administrator who is responsible for operating a hotline for residents. The working standards for a grid administrator are 'six knows', 'four arrives', 'four visits', and 'four reports'. The grid administrators are responsible for knowing the residents, staff, local facilities, hidden conflicts, and residents' needs and difficulties well. The grid administrators are also responsible for arriving promptly in case of emergencies, neighbourhood disputes, residents' misfortunes, and residents' appeals. They are responsible for visiting when residents are in difficulties or in great need of help, or if elderly or disabled people are living alone. The grid administrators are responsible for informing relevant departments in the case of hidden danger, unstable factors, unplanned birth, and residence changes. The performance of the grid administrators is evaluated according to residents' reviews and reports from relevant departments.

Urban Community Service in China

'Community service is helpful to facilitate the livelihood of the people' was written in the report of the Sixteenth National Congress of the CPC for the first time. Then *View on Strengthening and Improving Community Service* was issued by the State Council in April 2006. It proposed to establish a community service system, which would provide comprehensive social services and benefit all members of the community.

The Features of Community Service

China's community service is led by the CPC and government and is supported by non-governmental organisations, relevant government departments and their agencies, and residents' self-governing organisations. During the planned economy period, community service was provided in a top-down manner through government arrangements. As the social and economic transition has evolved, community service in China is more often provided through cooperation mechanisms among government, society, and the market. Government is still the main provider, but not the only one. Some non-governmental organisations, self-governing organisations, and private enterprises have begun to provide community service.

Current Development in Community Service

Since the mid-1980s, China's community service has experienced rapid development. It plays an important role in promoting economic development, maintaining social stability, and improving quality of life. At the end of 2010, there were 84,689 urban communities, 30,021 comprehensive community service stations, 3,515 street community service centres, and 693,000 public service outlets. Community health service centres, community cultural centres, and other special community service facilities have also been built. The implementation of a community volunteer registration system encourages the rapid development of community volunteer service. Supermarkets, vegetable markets, and breakfast stalls are priorities for support. Community services for the convenience of residents, such as housekeeping, property management, nurseries, repair services, and recycling services all feature in communities.

The number of people involved in community service is growing. It includes not only elected members of Residents' Committees but also full-time community workers. By the end of 2009, there were 431,000 members of Community Residents' Committees, 2.34 million members of Village Committees, and 2.158 million community workers. In addition, a growing number of residents become community volunteers, playing an active role in various fields of community service. The number of community volunteers reached 29 million by the end of 2009.

There is a 'one-stop' service in community service centres in some regions. Modern information technology has been applied to meet the needs of residents. Some local governments guide social organisations, enterprises, public institutions, and residents to participate in community administration and community service through government procurement. The service capacity of social organisations is thereby enhanced.

Although China's community service system has made considerable progress, there are still difficulties and problems. Many streets and communities still have a shortage of community service and facilities. For now, demand outstrips supply. The number and quality of social workers cannot meet needs. This can only be addressed by more volunteer community involvement.

The Developmental Direction of Urban Community Service

A Prerequisite of the Transformation of Government Functions

China's historical evolution and its administrative characteristics have put government in the central position to provide community service. The practice of government-oriented community service will continue. Sustained progress cannot be achieved in a relatively short period without

Figure 4.2: JingAn District Shi Men Er Road Sub-District Community Service Centre, Shanghai

government support. However, the absence and poor use of government resources in community service is increasingly obvious. Transformation of government functions is necessary and urgent. The government is trying to transition from 'unlimited government' to 'limited government'. The idea of limited government applied to community service is that new suppliers should be encouraged and fostered to take over many community service functions.

Non-governmental Organisations as the Carrier

The Chinese government is actively promoting non-governmental organisations (NGOs) to become the main suppliers of community service. The State Council highlighted the importance of developing NGOs in *View on Strengthening and Improving Community Service* (hereinafter referred to as the *View*) in April 2006.

The Basic Principles to Administer Non-governmental Organisations: Cultivation and Supervision

'Cultivation and supervision' means encouraging and supporting the development of NGOs. It also means strengthening their management in accordance with Chinese legislation. For example, Shanghai seeks to manage community NGOs through NGO service centres, which constitute a bridge between government and NGOs. The primary function of an NGO centre is to have a formal governmental influence over the local operation of NGOs. The staff of an NGO centre is recruited either by internal transfer (governmental) or open recruitment. The NGO centre is funded mainly by government procurement, supplemented by party membership dues of the CPC.

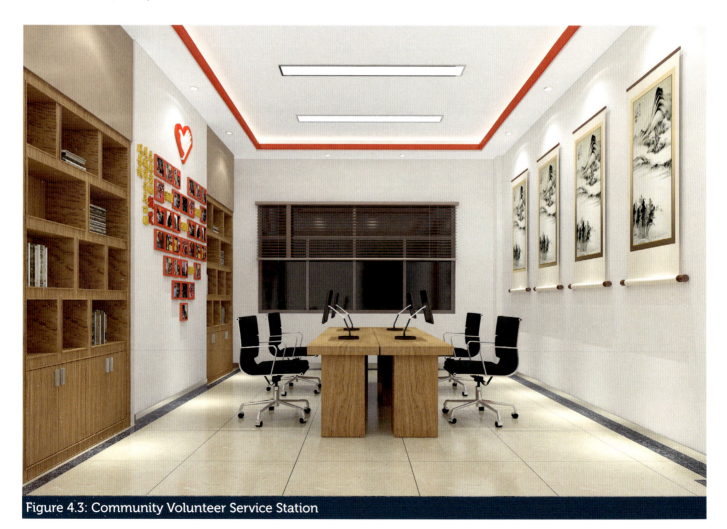

Figure 4.3: Community Volunteer Service Station

Community Residents' Self-governance in China

The Role of Community Residents' Self-governance

In China, modern community governance means close coordination among community units and the wide participation of residents under the guidance of the CPC. The long-term goal of community building is to realise Community Residents' Self-governance. 'Self-governance' was defined in *Options on Promoting Community Building*, issued by the Ministry of Civil Affairs in November 2000. Community Residents' Self-governance in China is neither federal nor local autonomy; instead it is a complement to government administration. Members of Community Residents' Committees are elected and are in charge of the daily affairs of communities. The Community Residents' Committee is a kind of self-governing organisation under the leadership of the CPC, through which residents handle their own affairs, educate themselves, and serve their own needs.[9]

The Functions of Community Residents' Self-governance[10]

The Residents' Committee is a self-governing organisation for the whole population. It assists the government in publicising the Constitution, laws, regulations, and state policies, protecting the lawful rights and interests of residents and educating residents in their statutory obligations. The committee assists the local government in the affairs of public health and poverty relief. According to the *Organic Law of the Urban Residents' Committees of PRC*, its self-governing functions include self-management, self-education, and self-service.

A Residents' Committee coordinates the relationship between government and residents. It also mediates disputes among the residents through its subcommittees, such as the People's Mediation Committee.[11] The Residents' Committee also has the responsibility to maintain public order. The Organic Law of Urban Residents' Committees clearly states that they can establish subcommittees for public security, whose task is to assist government to maintain public order.

Endnotes

1   Wang Zhenyao and Bai Yihua, eds, *Construction of Street Work and Residents' Committee*, China Social Sciences Press, 1996, pp. 179–181.

2   Lin Shangli (eds), *Community Organizations and Residents' Committee Building*, Shanghai: Shanghai University Press, 2001.

3   Chen Xian et al., *Community Economy and Community Service*, Shanghai: Shanghai University Press, 2001.

4   Ministry of Civil Affairs, *View on the Construction of Urban Communities Nationwide*, https://baike. so.com/doc/5119185-5348261.html (accessed 26 April 2018).

5   Decision of the CPC Central Committee on Major Issues Concerning the Construction of a Socialistic Harmonious Society, http://news.sina.com.cn/ c/2006-10-18/125711271474.shtml

6   Lu Hanlong, 'Organization construction of community service', *Quarterly Journal of Shanghai Academy of Social Sciences*, issue 2, 2002.

7   Ding Maozhan (ed.), *Administration System of Urban Community*, China Economic Publishing House, 2009, p. 52, Figure 2.1.

8   Liu Jun, 'A Survey Report of Grid Management in Hefei', Master's thesis, Anhui University, 2012.

9   Wang Bangzuo et al., *Residents' Committee and Community Governance: Urban Community Residents' Committee Organization*, Shanghai: Shanghai People's Publishing House, 2003.

10 Yu Yanyan, *Community Self-governance and Transformation of Government Functions*, Beijing: China Society Press, 2005.

11 The People's Mediation Committee is an organisation established in accordance with the law to mediate civil disputes. The People's Mediation Committee shall conduct its work under the guidance of local government and local courts. After mediation, relevant parties may reach a voluntary agreement and they have the duty to act according to the agreement. If they cannot reach a voluntary agreement, they bring a lawsuit to the people's court. The People's Mediation Committee is neither a kind of national judicial unit nor an administration organisation.

UNDERSTANDING THE ENVIRONMENTAL AGENDA

5

The Background of Ecological Civilisation

Macro Level: A National Philosophical Mindset

In 2007, at the Seventeenth National Congress of the CPC, the CPC stated that for the foreseeable future, China's economic model would be premised on the desire to create an 'Ecological Civilisation' (*shengtai wenming*, 生态文明). Soon after, the *China Daily* newspaper reported that ecological civilisation is 'a future-oriented guiding principle based on the perception of the extremely high price we have paid for our economic miracle'.[1] Put simply, the demands for an ecological civilisation, it said, were meant to herald a new epoch where social and economic development would continue but much more consideration would be given to its effects on people and the planet. China was one of the first countries in the developing world to strategically introduce sustainable development on a national and regional policy level.[2] China had rewritten its Constitution back in 1982 to include the pledge to 'protect the environment and natural resources by controlling pollution and its societal impact, ensure the sensible use of natural resources, and safeguard rare animals and plants'.[3] But even though significant environmental protection policies emerged from this pledge, China's waterways became more and more polluted,[4] heavy metal adulteration of rice crops is a cause for concern in southern China[5] and air quality

in certain cities has become a major issue. There is a clear recognition throughout the Chinese leadership that China's rapid economic development over the previous three decades has, in some ways, exacerbated industrial accidents. In the last 15 years, China has employed urgent remedial measures to rectify the situation. With reference to the deterioration in air quality for instance, in 2013 the Chinese State Council issued an Action Plan for the Prevention and Control of Air Pollution that aimed to reduce air pollution by over 10 per cent from 2012 to 2017.[6] It may not be enough, but measures like this and many others are focusing in the right direction.

The word *shengtai* (生态) – ecological – originates in scientific biology but has come into more common usage over the last decade to refer to the interdependency of all things.[7] Such interlinkages were spelled out by the Minister of Culture in 2007 and connected to issues of unspoiled, intangible cultural heritage. There are currently over 16 'eco-museums' for the 'protection of natural resources and the development of cultural identity', the first of which was set up among the remote Miao villages of Guizhou. The first eco-cultural protection zone was launched by the Vice Minister of Culture, Zhou Heping, in 2007 in Fujian, claiming that it would protect 'architecture, historical streets, and historical remains; and ... oral traditions, traditional performing arts, folk customs, rituals'.[8] Deputy Director of China's State Environmental Protection

Administration, Pan Yue, claims that China 'has maintained a nation state united by roots, language and ethnicity ... possible only because of the deep ecological wisdom contained within the country's cultural ideals'.[9] Even in relation to the cultural conceptualisation of ecology it often isn't clear which cultural heritage and which traditional wisdom is being referred to, and how 'intrinsic' these cultural values are. The Taoists' appreciation of nature as the source of moral understanding, for example, made sense for an ancient regime but is too impressionistic for China's contemporary needs. Consequently, there has arisen a preference for a more Confucian understanding of nature, which gives priority to the social affairs of man.[10]

Actually, for many years in post-war China, the political establishment tended to see human existence standing above nature, i.e., that humans had a civilising mission to tame nature for humanity's own purposes. In his article 'Ecological wisdom of the ages', Pan Yue notes that, 'China's adoption of the ecological agenda corrects the errors of consumerism and nihilism that western industrial civilisation has brought us'.[11] In this way, the Party has begun to use the rhetoric of ecology and sustainable development to promote national renewal and socialist ecological progress.[12]

Micro Level: Individual Behaviour Change

A second interpretation of the leadership's desire to create an eco-civilisation relates to the targeting of individual behaviour changes to encourage people to identify with a developed mentality. Back in 2003, the CPC wanted to create a 'well-off' society and cited that the new middle classes would be 'educated, cultured, civilized and creditable'.[13] The proposition was that economic advancement would cultivate more civilised behaviour, and encourage social refinement and environmental circumspection, all of which would freely emerge as the middle classes attained more leisure time and becoming more cultured. The new middle-class society would be one in which, it was argued, some are allowed to get rich first – a social experiment that would generate cultural pioneers whose wealth and breeding would trickle

Figure 5.1: Xijiang Qianhu Miao Village, National Eco-cultural Protection Zone, Guizhou Province

down to those who wait. The embodiment of this new cultivated society was the concept of *suzhi*, 素质, referring to the civilised behaviour standards of 'high quality people'.[14] Implicit in the success of this strategy is the belief that environmental conditions are a personal responsibility borne out of a full understanding of one's social duty.

So, we have two issues related to environmental remediation. On one hand, government clean-up campaigns; on the other, a notional environmental social contract. The former recognises the need of government and its representatives to ditch the rapacious. The latter points to the individual's and community's personal and social responsibilities to uplift themselves to a social standard of behaviour befitting a modern developed economy.

The Development of Chinese Eco-cities

The Definition of the Eco-city

A study by the People's Bank of China and the United Nations Environment Programme found that achieving the national targets for environmental clean-up, cutting emissions, investing in energy efficiency, and clean transportation will require an annual investment of at least CNY2 trillion (US$320 billion, or more than 3 per cent of GDP) for the next five years.[15] This is an unimaginably large investment – 20 times NASA's annual budget. As part of this process, President Xi co-drafted a declaration of environmental clean energy co-signed by President Obama to indicate the political seriousness with which China treats the environment.[16] Furthermore, a consortium comprising the People's Bank of China, the China Banking Regulatory Commission, the China Securities Regulatory Commission, and the China Insurance Regulatory Commission is being set up internally to 'work together with the government agencies to formulate financial policies that support the development of environmental service

industry'.[15] It is clear that ecology, environmental clean-up, and energy-saving are at the heart of China's development strategy and have been for some time.

Eco-cities will play a significant role. As early as 1995, the regulatory environmental agencies issued guidelines for proposed demonstration of eco-communities and environmental protection model cities under its Eco-Construction Programme. Subsequently, low-carbon eco-cities have been officially put forward as the answer to the PRC's urban development and environmental problems. Eco-cities cannot be built overnight: they require substantial technology (not just main infrastructure) and are often built on heavily remediated land away from existing centres.

The International Ecocity Frameworks and Standards (IEFS) has developed a global 'working definition' of an eco-city, coordinated through the United Nations' offices. The foundational group behind this initiative is Eco-city Builders founded by Richard Register – who reputedly first coined the term eco-city. The advisory body definition states that an eco-city is a human settlement that 'provides healthy abundance to its inhabitants without consuming more (renewable) resources than it produces, without producing more waste than it can assimilate, and without being toxic to itself or neighboring ecosystems'.[17] Many definitions exist and as a consequence Professor van Dijk authored a book called *Using 100 Criteria for the Classification of Ecological Cities*. Many definitions exist and Professor van Dijk states that, in practice, 'many cities claim to be ecological cities but there are no non-ambiguous definitions'.[18] There are, however, a huge array of measurement practices, each vying to be adopted as the benchmark. We will look at these later. In China, there are at least 40 presumed synonyms for eco-city such as green city, ecological city, liveable city, low-carbon city, and so on.

The Practices of Eco-cities

Around 200 significant eco-city projects have been proposed, are under construction, or have been partly or fully implemented across China.[19] According to the statistical data of the Chinese Urban Science Institute in 2011, which includes smaller-scale projects, there are 295 cities under so-called urban ecological construction.[20] This latter figure includes around 80 per cent prefecture-level cities (230), with 46 per cent (133) aiming to be specifically low-carbon cities.

Ren Xuefei, author of *Urban China*, notes that 'Eco-cities are intended to serve as role models for sustainable urban living in the future by experimenting with cutting edge technologies'.[21] Role models is a good way of characterising the eco-city phenomenon and on that basis, the idea is laudable: China is building places for people to live, work, and enjoy. They are doing so purposively, slowly, but they are building experimental urban centres to cater for the next influx of city aspirants. These are also places where China can try out new land-purchasing deals, liberalise planning constraints, and provide eco-inducements and lucrative commercial deals to foreign investors.

The University of Westminster has documented the various comparisons in urban sustainability frameworks often related to eco-city status, examining the different criteria demanded by a large number of major global authorities.[22] Table 5.1 shows a number of the criteria that Tianjin eco-city has to be assessed against. These framework rules and standards are set by the following site, local, provincial, state, and international indexing systems in order to qualify for Eco status.

Table 5.1: Comparisons in Urban Sustainability Frameworks

Name	Number of Indicators	'In Force' Date	Regulator	Notes
Eco-city Development Index System	2011	28	Chinese Society for Urban Studies	Proposed national indicator framework, organised along five categories and 28 indicators. Specific targets for the majority of indicators, with eight indicators defined more flexibly in terms of 'innovative approaches' and building on 2011.
Tianjin Binhai Eco-city	2010	26	Singapore and Chinese Governments	Key Performance Indicators with focus on resource efficiency. Incorporates Sino-Singaporean national standards and builds on earlier national frameworks.
National Eco-garden City	2010	19	China Ministry of Housing and Urban-Rural Development (MoHURD)	This is a national framework that comprises 19 indicators divided into three categories: natural environment, living environment, and infrastructure. Cities have to apply for renewal of 'National Eco-garden City' status every three years.
National Eco-county, Eco-city and Eco-province Indicators	2007	22	China Ministry of Environmental Protection	Framework of 22 indicators to assess cities' performance against standards. The indicators are divided into three categories: environment, economy, society.

The information in Table 5.1 has been gleaned from University of Westminster research.[23] This provides a glimpse of the huge amount of paperwork, monitoring, consultancy, and reporting – in other words, human time – spent accounting for this urban project.

Some areas are not weighed down in technical indices or are not designed to deal with people as residents. The Yangcheng Lake Renewal Project to the north of Suzhou, for instance, is a fine example of urban planning without the incursion of too many tick-box requirements. Vast areas of farmland and wetland have been upgraded to protect natural habitat, create a sensitive tourist playground and provide sanctioned fishing and recreational uses. It is a safe, secure, unpolluted, visual treat that is also, coincidentally, environmentally sensitive. But it is not a city. For that, you need people, transport, commerce, industry, a busy atmosphere, and a dynamic that introduces a *je ne sais quoi* into the equation.

In an eco-city, developers can experiment architecturally, universities can test new energy-saving designs and products; the government can develop cutting-edge testing processes to originate regulatory frameworks, and so on. In 2003, China's Ministry of Environmental Protection (MEP) initiated a programme to establish eco-counties, eco-cities, and eco-regions nationwide. Since getting that official sanction to proceed, the number of demonstration eco-projects has increased rapidly.[24] Up until July 2012, 97.6 per cent of prefecture-level cities and 80 per cent of county-level cities have proposed the goal of building an eco-city.[25] All the cities explored in this book's other chapters – Shanghai, Qingdao, Hangzhou, Hefei, Chengdu, and Nanchang – lay claim to some level of

Figure 5.2: Sino-Singapore Tianjin Eco-city

eco-development within their boundaries. All, to some extent, are trying something new in order to learn valuable lessons about quality, humane environments. The experiment is something akin to an urban scale version of the British Research Establishment (BRE), set up in the aftermath of the Second World War in the UK, to investigate the performance of various building materials and construction methods suitable for that fervid period of rapid house-building and urban reconstruction that was urgently needed after the devastation of the war. China is experiencing its own version of innovation and there is a similar need for efficiency frameworks, social improvements, infrastructure expansion, and urban experimentation. Chinese eco-cities are trying to differentiate themselves from the west, not least by the fact that they are building new cities and that they are well planned, financially backed, and prioritise the user – the resident, occupier, city dweller. In contract, the west regularly focuses on people as a problem (as James Lovelock says, 'the root cause is too many people … Just the

breathing those billions of people do … is a potent source of carbon dioxide').[26] Premier Li Keqiang stated in March 2013 that the new model of urbanisation should be human-centred and should ensure the prosperity of the people.[27]

Endnotes

1 Xinhua, 'Ecological civilization', *China Daily*, 24 October 2007, p. 10.

2 National Development and Reform Commission, *The People's Republic of China's Report on Sustainable Development*, NDRC, 2013, http://www.sdpc.gov.cn/xwzx/xwtt/t20120601_483687.htm (in Chinese) (accessed 28 April 2018).

3 Elisa Tsang in *Handbook of Global Environmental Policy and Administration*, eds Dennis L. Soden and Brent S. Steel. New York: Marcel Dekker, 1999, p. 383.

4 Elizabeth C. Economy, *The River Runs Black: The Environmental Challenge to China's Future*, Ithaca, NY: Cornell University Press, 2005.

5 B. Li, J. B. Shi, X. Wang, M. Meng, L. Huang, X. L. Qi, B. He, and Z. H. Ye, 'Variations and constancy of mercury and methylmercury accumulation in rice grown at contaminated paddy field sites in three Provinces of China', *Environmental Pollution*, Vol. 181, October 2013, pp. 91–97.

6 Philip Andrews-Speed, *China's Energy Policymaking Processes and their Consequences, The National Bureau of Asian Research Energy Security Report*. National Bureau of Asian Research, 2014.

7 Michael Dalton McCoy, *Domestic Policy Narratives and International Relations Theory: Chinese Ecological Agriculture as a Case Study*, Lanham, MD: University Press of America, 2003.

8 Keith Howard, *Music as Intangible Cultural Heritage: Policy, Ideology, and Practice in the Preservation of East Asian Traditions*, Farnham: Ashgate Publishing, 2012.

9 Pan Yue, 'Ecological wisdom of the ages', *China Dialogue*, 1 November 2011.

10 Mary Evelyn Tucker and John Berthrong, eds, *Confucianism and Ecology: The Interrelation of Heaven, Earth, and Humans*, Cambridge, MA: Harvard University Press, 1998.

11 Pan Yue, 'Ecological wisdom of the ages', *China Dialogue*, 1 November 2011.

12 Li Jie, 'The path, theory and system: The great innovation of socialism with Chinese characteristics', *Frontiers*, issue 12, 2012, Academy of Marxism, http://myy.cass.cn/ (accessed 4 October 2015).

13 Yingjie. Guo in David S. G. Goodman, *The New Rich in China: Future Rulers, Present Lives*, Abingdon: Routledge, 2008.

14 Julie Sze, *Fantasy Islands: Chinese Dreams and Ecological Fears in an Age of Climate Crisis*, Berkeley, CA: University of California Press, 2014.

15 People's Bank of China, United Nations Environment Programme, *Establishing China's Green Financial System: Report of the Green Finance Task Force*, 2015.

16 Office of the Press Secretary, *Fact Sheet: U.S.–China Joint Announcement on Climate Change and Clean Energy Cooperation*, The White House, 11 November 2014.

17 Definition as adopted by the International Ecocity Standards advisory team in Vancouver, Canada on 20 February 2010.

18 Meine Pieter van Dijk, 'Measuring eco cities, comparing European and Asian experiences: Rotterdam versus Beijing', *Asia-Europe Journal*, January 2015.

19 Chien Shiuh-Shen, 'Chinese eco-cities: A perspective of land-speculation-oriented local entrepreneurialism', *China Information*, 2013, pp. 173–196.

20 Na Kunpeng, 'Research on the development path of China's eco-city', *Urban Development Studies*, Vol. 20, issue 7, 2013, pp. 57–62.

21 Ren Xuefei, *Urban China*, Hoboken, NJ: John Wiley & Sons, 2013.

22 S. Joss, R. Cowley, M. de Jong, B. Muller, B-S. Park, W. Rees, M. Roseland, and Y. Rydin, *Tomorrow's City Today. Prospects for Standardizing Sustainable Urban Development*, London: University of Westminster, 2015.

23 Simon Joss and Daniel Tomozeiu, *'Eco-City' Frameworks – A Global Overview*, The Leverhulme International Network, 2013.

24 Nan Zhou, Gang He, and Christopher Williams, *China's Development of Low-carbon Eco-cities and Associated Indicator Systems*, Ernest Orlando Lawrence Berkeley National Laboratory, 2012.

25 Li Xun and Zhou Yan, 'The current situation, problems, solutions of Chinese eco-city development', *Urban Planning Journal*, issue 4, 2011, pp. 23–29.

26 James Lovelock, *The Vanishing Face of Gaia: A Final Warning*, London: Penguin, 2010.

27 Li Keqiang, 'Premier's press conference of the first session of the 12th National People's Congress', http://www.chinadaily.com.cn/dfpd/2013qglianghui/2013-03/17/content_16314456.htm (accessed 26 April 2018).

ASSESSMENT REPORT ON URBAN TRANSFORMATION AND UPGRADING CAPABILITIES IN CHINA

6

A Literature Review on Urban Transformation and Upgrading Research

The fields of urban transformation and upgrading have for some time been significant to both academic and policy study. More recently, such study has begun to address the challenges that have developed in the earlier period of industrialisation, such as resource shortage, environment deterioration, social tensions, the wide gap between rural and urban areas, and urbanisation lagging behind industrialisation. Here we explore the definition, pattern, and influential factors of urban transformation and upgrading in China.

The Content of Urban Transformation and Upgrading

In the early stages, scholars defined urban transformation mainly from political and economic perspectives. Gérard Roland asserts that transformation is a process of a large-scale institutional change.[1] Similarly, Wu proposed that urban transformation was relevant to land development and housing commercialisation and that it was fundamentally a political-economic process.[2] However, more recently a broader framework of factors has been identified. Urban development and transformation is interpreted as

a systematic process of continuous adjustments and improvement of urban systems which not only involves the transformation of urban economic, social, and ecological systems, but also the transformation of urban landscape and urban management systems.

Economic Transformation

Speeding up the economic transformation and improving the urban functions are key points in rejuvenating the urban development capacity. Urban economic transformation involves a series of structural changes in terms of industries, economic operating system, organisation, and management. Capital, technology, talents, and market are important influencing factors in urban economic transformation. Effective guidance and support from government can help to foster a favourable macroeconomic environment for urban economic transformation. The pattern of economic transformation includes industrial diversification, high-end orientation, and upgrading.[3] Based on the analysis of various industrial sectors on the outskirts of the Copenhagen metropolitan area, Hansen and Winther noted that the service economy is the dominant trajectory of urban economic transformation.[4] In order to fully grasp the nature and impact of urban transformation any performance evaluation system needs to examine not only objective criteria but also the subjective perception of urban dwellers.[5]

Social Transformation

Along with the rapid progress of urbanisation, the disequilibrium between rural areas and urban areas is widening, which affects the sustainable development of economy and society. Thus speeding up the process of urban social transformation is a decisive part in the construction of an overall well-off and innovative society. It is a precondition for further wealth creation in the countryside. As a start, social transformation means discovering fairer social welfare mechanisms with innovation in social security and fiscal policies such as income allocation and taxation management.

The essence of a harmonious urban society is improving people's lives and their sense of well-being. Public policies have decisive effects on urban social transformation, with decision makers always seeking to solve complex policy dilemmas.[6] For example, social welfare policies in some German cities have changed from 'employment centred' to 'family supporting' to reflect a much more embracing typology of social need. Some local governments in Germany offer transportation subsidies to inhabitants in order to increase the degree of population suburbanisation.[7, 8]

Cultural Transformation

As urbanisation intensifies, cultural life becomes a more important issue. There is a greater sensitivity to cultural institutions, value orientation, and historical background. Urban culture development is a strategic priority for urban regeneration in many European cities; for example, in London the cultural industries are one of three leading components for urban economic development.[9, 10]

A specific cultural institution, 'Cultiva', in the Norwegian city of Kristiansand has been set up to attract both investment and talent, as a core element for urban cultural and economic development.[11] The idea of the 'creative city' is now at the heart of many urban development plans.[12]

Ecological Transformation

Environmental problems such as global warming and resource exhaustion have become severe challenges for urban sustainable development. Ecological transformation must try to establish a sustainable development mode that emphasises improving environment quality, protecting natural landscapes, keeping ecological balance, and increasing residential habitability. There are already many international examples to consider. For instance, Baltimore's Inner Harbor has been modified into a sightseeing destination through ecological transformation, displaying a development mode from industrial civilisation to ecological civilisation.[13] From the perspective of urban ecological transformation, domestic Chinese scholars have studied environmental protection and ecological transformation measures such as creating green residential environments in order to change the urban–rural dual structure.[14]

Main Patterns of Urban Transformation and Upgrading

Headquarters Economy Pattern

The headquarters of high-end industries are located in the city centre, while manufacturing and processing at the low end of the value chain are usually located in less developed cities. The siting of headquarters can not only help big cities to gain a resource advantage but can also help them to realise economic transformation by enhancing their economic drive and radiation capabilities – the impact they have on the surrounding area. Currently, several Chinese cities have entered into the development stage of a headquarters economy.[15]

Knowledge City Pattern

This essentially means redefining an urban area that already has important attributes such as universities and available land for new start-ups and cultural locations as knowledge hubs. The land and buildings are usually recycled from redundant industrial and warehouse sites.[16] A notable example is Melbourne – designating itself as a learning society, it gets a competitive boost by attracting high-quality talent, and a wide spectrum of cultural industries and activities. It is summed up as a human-centred city in Melbourne Planning (2010) and Melbourne Urban Strategy (2030).[17]

Following this example, the city of Shenzhen has implemented new 'branding': once it was 'assembled' or 'made' in Shenzhen, now it is 'Invented in Shenzhen'.

Ecological City Pattern

If the earlier patterns have become embedded in urban development then in a post-industrial economy a pattern of recycling becomes more feasible. A recycling pattern helps to reduce economic cost by combining enhanced economic performance with a positive environmental effect.[18] Components of this pattern include establishing a recycling system both for industry and domestic consumption.[19] This pattern of development has taken hold since the 1980s, concentrated around environmental beautification and resource recycling.[20]

Evaluation Indices for Urban Sustainable Development

Since the 1990s, scholars have sought to measure sustainable urban transformation through various sets of criteria, often in the form of an urban index, each with a set of concepts, principles, and frameworks. These have been essentially quantitative in methodology.

Using the BP Neural Network model, Zhu Mingfeng, Hong Tianqiu, and Ye Qiang analysed the economy and sustainable development situation in some resource-based cities.[21] By using the Ecological Footprint Theory, Zang Shuying, Zhi Ruizhi, and Sun Xuemeng analysed the ecological footprint of the city of Daqing from 1980 to 2001, and gave a quantitative evaluation report of the sustainable development capability of the city.[22]

However, many studies in the field of urban sustainable development evaluation give no more than a suggestion about their index system and evaluation method. They are not able to provide relevant empirical analysis. The evaluation index systems are mainly constructed from two perspectives: that of the economy, society, environment, and resources, or that of development and coordination levels. Most of the studies are focused on the analysis of urban industrial structure and are not perfect in the analysis of industry choice. In terms of research method, most of the studies are descriptive, and lack in-depth empirical analysis.[23]

Factors to Influence Urban Transformation and Upgrading

Wei Lihua, Lu Ming, and Yan Xiao Pei argue that in the early period of urbanisation it is the transition from an agricultural to an industrial economy that drives change.[24] During this transition, urbanisation is the key means to realising social transformation, while industrialisation is the fundamental driving force to realise urbanisation. This may be an adequate description of an earlier period but Zhu Tiezhen points out that as the city develops the process of urban transformation is actually a process of urban innovation. Without innovation, the functions of cities cannot be improved, strengthened, and diversified.[25] Ye Yumin and Tang Jie stress the importance of leading industries in urban transformation. They assert that urban transformation depends on economic adaptation and replacement of the previously leading industries.[26]

From a geographical perspective, Chai Yanwei and Zhang Chun study the transformation from 'unit people' to 'community people' and suggest that urban spatial transition comes after the social transition.[27] Considering urban transformation as the deepening of urbanity, Li Yanjun points out that urban transformation involves both economic transformation and, increasingly, social transformation.[28]

Urban transformation in China demonstrates three interrelated and supportive pillars: industrial transformation, a growing middle class, and institutional innovation. Industrial transformation supports economic transformation, the rise of the middle class supports social transformation, and institutional innovation provides a guarantee for economic and social transformation.

Wei Houkai believes that the driving factors of urban transformation must include: the mindset of urban development, the stage of urban development, resource endowment, technology, and consumption demand.[29] Wu Fulong points out that urban transformation is the result of interaction between internal and external factors. External factors involve the change of production mode from Fordism to post-Fordism, the appearance of a more specialised production system, diversified consumer demand, and the rapid global expansion of capital.[30] The internal factors stem from local government policy, the activities and aspirations of citizens, and the sense of how liveable the city is. Logan emphasises the importance of globalisation. He claims there are three driving forces of urban transformation: market-oriented institutional transformation, rural-urban transition, and the forces of globalisation.[31]

Critical Mass in Urban Transformation and Upgrading Capability

Urban transformation and upgrading should develop an incremental and self-development capacity as proposed by Lin Yifu.[32] Following on from this, Li Qingchun proposed that this internal dynamic become a prerequisite for sustained urban transformation.[33] Wang Ke broadened this idea by suggesting that this applies at a regional level – a totality of natural and social productivity in a region covering the natural, material, human, and social capital.[34] Cen Jie et al. pointed out that regional self-development ability is the overall capacity for sustainability in the region, which embraces resource integration, innovation, and operational abilities.[35]

Michael Porter proposed the Diamond Model, which helps to explain systematically urban transformation and upgrading capabilities.[36] Porter proposes that the following four factors can decide the competitiveness of a specific industry or country:

- Production factors – including human resources, natural resources, knowledge resources, capital resources, and infrastructure.

- Demand factors – mainly domestic demand.

- The performance of relevant and supportive industries – whether these possess international competitiveness is of great significance.

- Strategies and competition structure – the performance of any given city is measured against that of its competitors.

Porter suggests that these four factors are interactive, forming a diamond system (Figure 6.1). Around the factors, there are two variables: government and opportunity. Opportunity is less controllable but initiative can be taken and opportunities seized, and this is where the influence of government policies should not be ignored.

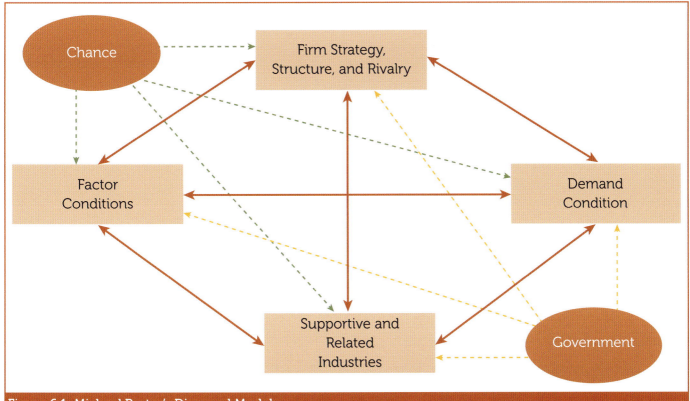

Figure 6.1: Michael Porter's Diamond Model

In summary, Urban Transformation and Upgrading Capability refers to the capacity for the integration, organisation, and allocation of a totality of resources: natural, material, human, cultural, and social, within the region. It also addresses the relationship to the external environment based on regional location advantage and resource endowment.

The Evaluation Model of Urban Transformation and Upgrading Capability in China

The Principles for Selecting the Index

The Urban Transformation and Upgrading Capability index for China developed in CELAP is based on existing research. The principles for selecting the specific indicators are 'scientific', 'critical', and 'practical'. The index system corresponds to the theory and evaluation method of city transformation outlined earlier. The index indicators are concise and representative enough to describe the overall situation. They are also accessible, so that we can continuously monitor the evolutionary trend of Chinese Urban Transformation and Upgrading Capability.

The Original Version of the Evaluation Index

The research team sent questionnaires to relevant experts and acquired anonymous feedback from them. And then, we formed a panel of experts to discuss the index system. We set up the original version of the index system including 22 indicators (see Table 6.1). In order to set up a fair and objective evaluation system, the original data for these indices came from the *China Urban Statistical Yearbook 2012*. We obtained all the 22 indicators for the 287 cities on China's mainland for 2011. Since we cannot get the relevant data for the city of Lhasa in the Tibet Autonomous Region, this is not included in the ranking and evaluation. We used principal component analysis to process the data. By using the dimension reduction method, principal component analysis can convert multiple factors into a few comprehensive factors.

Table 6.1: The Evaluation Index of Chinese Urban Transformation and Upgrading Capability (Original Version)

Indicators	Unit of Measurement	Notes
Proportion of the Tertiary Industry to GDP	%	
GDP Growth Rate	%	
Expenditure Percentage on Science and Technology	%	
Expenditure Percentage on Education	%	
Registered Urban Unemployment Rate	%	
Employment Percentage in the Tertiary Industry	%	
Employment Percentage in the Information Industry Compared to that in the Tertiary Industry	%	
Profit Rate of the Industrial Sector	%	
Profit Rate of Fixed Assets in the Industrial Sector	%	
Comprehensive Utilisation Rate of Industrial Solid Waste	%	
Recovery Rate of Industrial Sulphur Dioxide	%	
Removal Rate of Industrial Soot and Dust	%	
Green Coverage Ratio of the Built-up Area	%	
Per Capita GDP	CNY10,000/people	
Volume of Posts and Telecommunications Service Per Capita	Yuan/people	
Loan Balance of Financial Institutions	CNY10,000	
Amount of Foreign Investment Actually Utilised	US$10,000	
Urban Road Area Per Capita	Km^2/people	
Duration of Air Quality up to API 100 Standard	Days	
Discharge Volume of Industrial Waste Water	10,000 MT	Negative Utility Index
Industrial Power Consumption Per CNY10,000 Output Value	kW-hours/CNY10,000 Output Value	Negative Utility Index
Industrial Water Consumption Per CNY10,000 Output Value	MT/CNY10,000 Output Value	Negative Utility Index

With indicators for 287 cities (except Lhasa of the Tibet Autonomous Region) as samples, we set up a matrix with the standardised data variables of the 22 indicators and applied statistical software SPSS 18.0 to process the data. The testing coefficient of Kaiser-Meyer-Olkin (KMO) Measure of Sampling Adequacy is 0.769 (bigger than 0.7), which means the data is suitable for factor analysis. The testing coefficient of Bartlett's test of sphericity also shows that the data is suitable for factor analysis. According to the connotation of the self-development ability, we selected the principal components based on the criterion that matrix Eigenvalue is greater than 1.

Eight Eigenvalues were selected as principal components, with accumulative variance up to 65.021 per cent. Since the obtained factor cannot sufficiently reflect the index information of principal components, we use the varimax rotation method to acquire extraction results and regression coefficient, so the principal components are determined (see Table 6.2).

Table 6.2: Matrix of Rotation Components

	Main Components							
	1	2	3	4	5	6	7	8
Loan Balance of Financial Institutions	.911	.032	-.012	.154	.006	.016	-.058	.042
Amount of Foreign Investment Actually Utilised	.904	.021	-.046	.061	-.009	-.030	-.032	-.028
Discharge Volume of Industrial Waste Water	-.627	-.099	-.009	.155	-.220	-.083	-.217	.044
Expenditure Percentage on Science and Technology	.601	.416	.057	-.154	.166	-.040	.093	-.070
Green Coverage Ratio of Built-up Area	.031	.746	-.047	.010	-.023	.104	.051	-.054
Volume of Posts and Telecommunications Service Per Capita	.508	.648	.053	.054	.015	.048	-.089	.019
Profit Rate of the Industrial Sector	-.114	-.100	.867	.164	-.089	.139	.024	.019
Profit Rate of Fixed Assets in the Industrial Sector	.050	.009	.738	-.047	-.020	.072	.374	-.095
Urban Road Area Per Capita	.190	.412	.416	-.197	.283	-.356	.015	.044
Per Capita GDP	.402	.303	.416	-.362	.238	-.269	-.191	.076
Employment Percentage in the Tertiary Industry	-.142	-.118	.087	.848	-.123	.025	.074	.022
Proportion of the Tertiary Industry Compared to GDP	.356	.163	-.023	.714	.132	.024	.052	.142
Recovery Rate of Industrial Sulphur Dioxide	.098	.105	-.173	.027	.736	-.070	.096	-.165
Removal Rate of Industrial Soot and Dust	.039	-.011	.093	-.060	.699	.042	-.023	.120
Duration of Air Quality up to API100 Standard	-.158	.295	.016	.022	-.420	-.138	.377	.041
Expenditure Percentage on Education	-.179	-.036	.073	.195	.070	.777	.016	-.142
Registered Urban Unemployment Rate	.224	.161	.135	-.159	-.058	.629	-.128	.111
GDP Growth Rate	-.191	-.335	.142	.273	-.110	-.339	-.087	-.105
Industrial Power Consumption Per CNY10,000 Output Value	.059	.048	.175	.161	.019	-.076	.770	.013
Industrial Water Consumption Per CNY10,000 Output Value	.012	-.364	.117	-.326	.165	.218	.451	.179
Employment Percentage in the Information Industry Compared to that in the Tertiary Industry	.085	-.047	.014	.081	-.083	-.062	.209	.817
Comprehensive Utilisation Rate of Industrial Solid Waste	.227	-.002	.094	-.014	-.103	-.062	.412	-.617

Extraction Method: Principal Component Analysis.
Rotation Method: Varimax Rotation with Kaiser Normalisation.

a. Rotation Converged in Eight Iterations.

From Table 6.2, we can discern:

■ The load coefficients with higher absolute value from the first principal component are: the loan balances of financial institutions, amount of foreign investment actually utilised, expenditure percentage on science and technology, discharge volume of industrial waste water. In summary, they represent regional financing capability and science and innovation capability.

- The second principal component shows green coverage of built-up areas, volume of posts, and telecommunications service per capita. These factors represent the situation for the ecological environment and the penetration levels of communication service.

- The third principal component shows the profit rate in the industrial sector, for fixed assets in the industrial sector, urban road area per capita and per capita GDP. These represent the overall urban development level and industrial development efficiency.

- The fourth principal component shows employment percentage in the tertiary sector and the proportion of the tertiary sector in the GDP. This represents the urban economy structure.

- The fifth principal component shows the recovery rate of industrial sulphur dioxide, removal rate of industrial soot and dust, and duration of air quality up to API100 standard. These represent the degree of ecological and resource-intensive utilisation.

- The sixth principal component shows the expenditure percentage on education, registered urban unemployment rate and GDP growth rate. These represent human capital capability.

- The seventh principal component shows industrial power consumption per CNY10,000 output value, industrial water consumption per CNY10,000 output value, and comprehensive utilisation rate of industrial solid waste. These represent the capability to effectively use industrial resources.

- The eighth principal component shows the employment percentages in the information industry within the broader tertiary sector industry. This represents the urban informatisation level.

The Revised Version of the Evaluation Index

Index System

Our research team gave the original version of the index system and the analysis results for the eight principal components to a panel of experts and acquired anonymous feedback. We held a series of seminars to discuss and modify the original version of the index.

In order to continuously analyse and evaluate the Urban Transformation and Upgrading Capability in China, the index contains five secondary indexes with 28 third-grade indicators. The secondary indexes are comprehensive economic development capability, scientific and technical innovation capability, urban development effectiveness, suitability for living, and entrepreneurship and financing capability.

Although principal component factor analysis can convert the multiple factors to a few representative comprehensive factors, and determine the weight according to the variance, it is difficult for the method to track and compare the analysis results in different years. This is because the representative factors and weights calculated from the data of different years vary and are not comparable. In order to continuously track and compare, we assessed the analysis result based on 2011's data, and modified the original version of the index system. The revised version of the index system is in Table 6.3.

Data Source

In order to carry out a fair and objective evaluation, we took the data to make 26 indicators from the *China Urban Statistical Yearbook*. The data of a number of listed companies in the Small and Medium Enterprise Board and Growth Enterprises Market is quoted from public data released by the China Securities Regulatory Commission. The data for the number of companies selected from the 500 most valuable companies in China is quoted

Table 6.3 The Evaluation Index of Chinese Urban Transformation and Upgrading Capability (Revised Version)

	Weight	Indicator	Unit of Measurement	Weight	Notes
Comprehensive Economic Development Capability	27%	Per Capita GDP	CNY10,000 CNY/person	5%	
		GDP Growth Rate	%	5%	
		Proportion of the Tertiary Industry Compared to GDP	%	5%	
		Growth Rate of Fiscal Revenue	%	7%	
		Proportion of the GDP from the Modern Service Industry Compared to that from the Tertiary Industry	%	5%	
Scientific and Technical Innovation Capability	25%	Expenditure Percentage on Science and Technology	%	5%	
		Expenditure Percentage on Education	%	4%	
		Proportion of R&D Investment to GDP	%	5%	
		Number of Invention Patents Ownership for Every 10,000 People	Number of Pieces/10,000 People	5%	
		Number of Listed Companies in Small and Medium Enterprise Board and Growth Enterprises Market	Number of Companies	3%	
		Number of Companies Selected by the List of the 500 Most Valuable Companies in China	Number of Companies	3%	
Urban Development Effectiveness	18%	Per Unit Area GDP	CNY10,000/ 1 km²	3%	
		Growth Rate of Permanent Population	%	3%	
		Profit Rate of the Industrial Sector	%	2%	
		Profit Rate of Fixed Assets in the Industrial Sector	%	2%	
		Industrial Power Consumption Per CNY10,000 Output Value	kW-hour/ CNY10,000 Output Value	2%	Negative Utility Index
		Industrial Water Consumption Per RMB10,000 Output Value	Ton/ CNY10,000 Output Value	2%	Negative Utility Index
		Comprehensive Utilisation Rate of Industrial Solid Waste	%	2%	
		Urban Per Capita Disposable Income	CNY	2%	

Continued overleaf ...

	Weight	Indicator	Unit of Measurement	Weight	Notes
Suitability for Living and Entrepreneurship	20%	Duration of Air Quality up to API100 Standard	Number of Days	2%	
		Recovery Rate of Industrial Sulphur Dioxide	%	2%	
		Removal Rate of Industrial Soot and Dust	%	2%	
		Green Coverage Ratio of Built-up Area	%	3%	
		Urban Road Area Per Capita	m²/per capita	3%	
		Average Number of Hospital Beds for Every 10,000 People	Number of Beds/10,000 People	3%	
		Employment Rate	%	5%	
Financing Capability	10%	Loan Balance of Financial Institutions	CNY10,000	5%	
		Amount of Foreign Investment Actually Utilised	US$10,000	5%	

from the rank list released by the World Brand Lab. We then collected all the data for 28 indicators for 289 cities on the Chinese mainland.

Non-dimensionalisation of Data

We introduced non-dimensionalisation to eliminate the influences derived from dimension differences of these 28 indicators. The common methods of non-dimensionalisation include utility value treatment, standardisation treatment, and functional treatment. We adopted the utility value treatment method to remove the influence of non-standardised dimensions in indicators. The range of utility value is 0.100, with maximum utility value of 100 and minimum of 0. Since the influence of the indicator with positive utility values is the opposite of the indicator with negative utility values, the non-dimensionalisation treatment formulas are different:

When V_{ij} is a positive utility indicator, the higher the original value, the higher the utility value.

$$Y_{ij} = \frac{V_{ij} - V_{imin}}{V_{imax} - V_{imin}} *100$$

When V_{ij} is a negative utility indicator, the higher the original value, the lower the utility value.

$$Y_{ij} = \frac{V_{imax} - V_{ij}}{V_{imax} - V_{imin}} *100$$

Y_{ij} represents the utility value of i indicator from evaluation object j.

V_{ij} represents the original data of i indicator from evaluation object j.

V_{imax} represents the maximum value among all the original values of i indicator.

V_{imin} represents the minimum value among all the original values of i indicator.

The Ranking of China's Urban Transformation and Upgrading Capability

Using the indicators for 289 cities we built a matrix with the standardised data variables, applying statistical software SPSS 18.0 to process the data. On the basis of this comprehensive evaluation we ranked the top ten cities at sub-provincial and municipality level, and the top ten cities at prefecture level (see, respectively, Tables 6.4 and 6.5). Since we cannot obtain the relevant data for Haidong in Qinghai Province, this city is not included in the ranking and evaluation.

From 2012 to 2014, Beijing, Shenzhen, and Shanghai were the top three cities in the same ranking order. Nanjing, Hangzhou, Guangzhou, Tianjin, and Chengdu were among the top ten cities for all three of these years. There was intense competition for fourth place. Hangzhou ranked fourth in 2012, Guangzhou in 2013, and Nanjing in 2014.

From the view of spatial distribution, the top ten cities at sub-provincial and municipal level and the top ten at prefecture level were mainly located in the east of China. Chengdu and Wuhan were the only two cities represented from the Central, Western, and Northeast regions of China, at sub-provincial and municipal level. Chengdu ranked eighth place in all three years. Wuhan only ranked number ten in a single year, 2012.

The dominance of the eastern seaboard was even more pronounced in the ranking of prefecture-level cities. Kunming was the only city from the Central, Western, and Northeast regions of China, and entered the top ten in 2012.

The centres of urban development at present remain in and around the Yangtze River Delta, the Pearl River Delta, and Beijing–Tianjin–Hebei Region. The Yangtze River Delta has the most competitive strength and plays a strategic role. From 2012 to 2014, besides Shanghai, Hangzhou in Zhejiang Province and Nanjing in Jiangsu Province were among the top ten cities at sub-provincial level. From 2012 to 2014, Suzhou, Wuxi, Changzhou, and Zhenjiang, also in the Yangtze River Delta, were among the top ten cities at prefecture level. In addition, Nantong was in the top ten at prefecture level in 2012 and 2013. Shaoxing was among the top ten at prefecture level in 2013.

Table 6.4: Top Ten Cities of Urban Transformation and Upgrading Capability among Sub-provincial Cities and Municipalities

Ranking	Sub-provincial and Municipalities (2012)	Sub-provincial and Municipalities (2013)	Sub-provincial and Municipalities (2014)
1	Beijing	Beijing	Beijing
2	Shenzhen	Shenzhen	Shenzhen
3	Shanghai	Shanghai	Shanghai
4	Hangzhou	Guangzhou	Nanjing
5	Nanjing	Hangzhou	Hanghzou
6	Tianjin	Nanjin	Guangzhou
7	Dalian	Tianjin	Tianjin
8	Chengdu	Chengdu	Chengdu
9	Guangzhou	Qingdao	Xiamen
10	Wuhan	Changsha	Ji'nan

Table 6.5: Top Ten Cities of Urban Transformation and Upgrading Capability among Prefecture-level Cities

Ranking	Prefecture-level Cities (2012)	Prefecture-level Cities (2013)	Prefecture-level Cities (2014)
1	Suzhou	Suzhou	Suzhou
2	Wuxi	Wuxi	Dongguan
3	Dongguan	Dongguan	Wuxi
4	Changzhou	Changzhou	Zhuhai
5	Foshan	Zhuhai	Changzhou
6	Zhongshan	Foshan	Haikou
7	Zhenjiang	Nantong	Zhenjiang
8	Zhuhai	Zhongshan	Foshan
9	Xiamen	Zhenjiang	Kunming
10	Nantong	Shaoxing	Shantou

The Pearl River Delta region is the pioneer of reform and opening-up, and is at the same time one of the main economic centres. Shenzhen and Guangzhou were among the top ten cities at sub-provincial level in all three years. Dongguan, Foshan, and Zhuhai were among the top ten cities at prefecture-level in all three years. Zhongshan made the top ten at prefecture level in 2012 and 2013, and Shantou was among the top ten cities in 2014. Hong Kong and Macao were not included in the ranking. Hong Kong, Macao, and Guangzhou are at the centre of the Pearl River Delta region, while Shenzhen, Foshan, and Zhuhai are important sub-centres.

Xiamen, the capital of Fujian Province, to the north of Guangdong on the eastern seaboard, was in the top ten sub-provincial cities. The cities in Fujian Province with the new opportunities of a Free Trade Area and as part of the Sea Silk Road strategy are well placed to move up the rankings.

The Beijing–Tianjin–Hebei region is the largest city agglomeration in North China, and the gateway for the opening-up of this area. From 2012 to 2014, Beijing took first position in the ranking list, and Tianjin was also among the top ten. However, these advanced large cities are surrounded by a backward hinterland – this is the main issue to be addressed in the region.

In Hebei Province, only four of 11 cities (Shijiazhuang, Langfang, Qinhuangdao, and Handan) were among the top 100 cities at prefecture level. On 30 April 2015, the Political Bureau of the CPC Central Committee held a meeting to examine and approve the Plan for the Coordinated Development in Beijing–Tianjin–Hebei Area. This means the coordinated development of Beijing, Tianjin, and Hebei is now a national strategy. The core is to shift the non-capital functions of Beijing. Breakthroughs are expected to be made in the field of transport integration, ecological environment protection, industrial upgrading, and transfer. On 1 April 2017, China announced the plan to create the Xiongan New Area in Hebei Province. The launch of this new area is expected to host some of Beijing's non-capital functions, to explore a new model of optimised development in densely populated areas, and to restructure the urban layout in the Beijing–Tianjin–Hebei Region.

Cities in China's central region are now developing rapidly, and their urban transformation capability has improved, but compared with the cities in the eastern region their overall competitiveness is still weak. Changsha was the only city among the top ten cities of sub-provincial and municipal status in 2013.

The western region is richly endowed with natural resources and its market potential is promising. Although the western region has a crucial strategic position especially in relation to the One Belt and One Road Initiative, it must overcome the legacy of its historic underdevelopment and isolation. In recent years, more rapid development has taken place, mainly in Chengdu–Chongqing, Guanzhong–Tianshui, and the Ring Beibu Gulf Region. As noted, Chengdu was among the top ten cities in this period.

In the same region Chongqing, an inland port on the Yangtze River, has built on its historic role as a political, economic, cultural, and social centre but it has yet to reach the top ten. Chongqing was the seventeenth in the ranking of the sub-provincial cities; and around fiftieth across the whole ranking (forty-sixth in 2012, fifty-second in 2013, and forty-eighth in 2014).

Heavy industry developed first in Northeast China. However, in recent years, this old Rust Belt economy has experiencing a sharp recession and it has become a region with a net outflow of population. Dalian was the only city that was among the top ten cities at sub-provincial level in 2012, and has been the most successful in upgrading the economic structure.

In 2011, the urbanisation rate in China passed 50 per cent. By 2014, the rate reached 54.77 per cent. Major changes have taken place in the urban spatial patterns and the urban system. The mere input of economic factors is no longer enough to achieve sustainable urbanisation. New problems and challenges must be met.

Location, size, and structure determine the possibilities for enhanced urbanisation. Cities must accelerate using technology and innovation: a shift from a factor-driven mode to an innovation-driven one. Urban development must be transformed from extensive to intensive growth. The cities in the eastern coastal region, starting from a higher base, will have to lead this. Metropolises such as Beijing and Shanghai are facing an increasing population pressure, which intensifies the tension between developmental potential and comprehensive carrying capacity.

During the transformation from the planned economy to the market economy, most cities in China mainly relied on low-cost activities. With the comparative advantage of cheap labour, they drew in low-end manufacturing from all over the world. In the present circumstances, further change must confront the first-mover advantage in developed countries and also late-mover advantages in more recently developing countries. Cities such as Suzhou, Dongguan, and Foshan, which prospered in the earlier phase as export-oriented cities, need to adopt a strategy of high-end innovation.

The need for ecological transformation is compelling. The ultimate purpose of the city is to improve quality of life, and to offer harmony between people and the natural environment. In recent years, although efforts have been made to protect the environment, pollution problems are still serious. Beijing took the number one position in the index but throughout the year citizens have to cope with 'fog and haze' and sandstorms from the north. Administrative means are useful in the short run, but they just scratch the surface of this problem. So, the governance of fog and haze requires long-term planning and implementation. It is possible to achieve the dual goals of economic development and pollution reduction with the help of technological progress and institutional regulation.

Cities face sometimes crisis levels of exhaustion of resources. Resource-based cities all over the world generally experience a common evolution: an initial stage, development stage, prosperity stage, declining stage, and fading-away stage. In China, most resource-based cities have experienced the stages of 'exploiting resources, building industrial bases, forming urban cities'.[37] For too long they have relied on just a few natural resources, which has deformed the economic structure. Such cities are confronted with the following problems: exhaustion of resources, imperfect industrial chain, environmental deterioration, and vulnerable sustainable development capability.

The financial capability of local government is a critical foundation for urban transformation and upgrading, and in turn, successful transformation and upgrading is helpful to improve solvency. Local government spending has played an important role in accelerating urban transformation, infrastructure construction, and improving people's livelihood, but at the expense of heavy local debt. Many local governments rely on the income from land transfer to promote urbanisation and transformation, which also exacerbates the problem of local debt. On 30 December 2013, the National Audit Office issued a national audit report of local governments. At the end of June 2013, the total amount of debts that local governments had to repay was up to CNY10.88 trillion. The total amount of debt that local governments had to guarantee liability for was up to CNY2.66 trillion, and the total amount of contingent liability that local governments had part of salvage obligation for was up to CNY4.33 trillion. Generally speaking, the risks of government debts in China are under control because of the huge reserves at the centre, but there are hidden financial troubles in some cities. The Chinese government now seeks to carry out public–private partnerships (PPPs), and to replace the high-interest loans with low-interest local treasury bonds in order to ease the financial burden on local government.[38]

Table 6.6: Comprehensive Ranking of China's Urban Transformation and Upgrading Capability (2012–14)

Ranking	2013	Total Score	2014	Total Score	2015	Total Score
1	Beijing	53.96832839	Beijing	51.55870259	Beijing	55.04553112
2	Shenzhen	46.86223351	Shenzhen	49.20333587	Shenzhen	44.43694922
3	Shanghai	44.41481204	Shanghai	41.41031101	Shanghai	40.88577954
4	Suzhou	44.33110533	Suzhou	41.29291182	Suzhou	37.34079676
5	Hangzhou	39.88677854	Guangzhou	37.59511266	Nanjing	34.48569327
6	Wuxi	39.16012035	Hangzhou	36.18209911	Hangzhou	34.41009705
7	Dongguan	37.82991839	Wuxi	35.90346967	Dongguan	34.20482628
8	Nanjing	37.42807448	Dongguan	35.39057077	Guangzhou	33.71894574
9	Tianjing	36.80498292	Nanjing	35.10303204	Tianjing	33.41322845
10	Dalian	36.18154816	Tianjing	34.64160902	Wuxi	33.35640643
11	Chengdu	35.35727377	Changzhou	33.31658241	Zhuhai	31.13717152
12	Guangzhou	35.03769391	Zhuhai	32.26473144	Chengdu	31.1074978
13	Changzhou	34.72566576	Chengdu	32.18360537	Xiamen	31.0123127
14	Wuhai	34.31717509	Qingdao	31.5650286	Changzhou	30.94982327
15	Foshan	34.08387705	Foshan	31.3797416	Jinan	30.84610902
16	Zhongshan	33.96140821	Changsha	31.23934459	Haikou	30.79089537
17	Zhenjiang	33.53864708	Nantong	31.2248049	Zhenjiang	30.40135928
18	Changsha	33.39099359	Zhongshan	30.99707251	Qingdao	30.25847617
19	Shenyang	33.37604696	Zhenjiang	30.83950914	Foshan	30.23207158
20	Qingdao	33.35545263	Jinan	30.81531658	Kunming	29.66853072
21	Jinan	33.09717544	Wuhan	30.70359758	Changsha	29.64569761
22	Zhuhai	32.99496946	Xiamen	30.46407825	Shantou	29.48191756
23	Xiamen	32.95770372	Ningbo	30.33715721	Wuhan	29.46190022
24	Nantong	32.9433325	Dalian	30.30506964	Weifang	29.30881593
25	Suqian	32.64369259	Shaoxing	30.26082041	Zhongshan	29.25022396
26	Ningbo	32.59672649	Wenzhou	29.96303244	Wenzhou	29.07574298
27	Shaoxing	32.47295369	Weifang	29.94679197	Shaoxing	29.07458147
28	Hefei	32.17506366	Jiaxing	29.93693384	Jiaxing	29.0156754
29	Jinhua	32.1739029	Jinhua	29.86726651	Nantong	28.83860486
30	Xuzhou	31.90530058	Huzhou	29.62848608	Jinhua	28.75464826
31	Yulin	31.729074	Xi'an	29.1905295	Guiyang	28.73317157
32	Ordos	31.70576911	Yantai	29.14774759	Ningbo	28.55873733
33	Jiaxing	31.60701198	Zibo	29.1010661	Dongying	28.47398386

Ranking	2013	Total Score	2014	Total Score	2015	Total Score
34	Taiyuan	31.49365106	Fuzhou	29.05175206	Yulin	28.44288701
35	Dongying	31.43433775	Yangzhou	29.03189186	Taizhou	28.39640741
36	Zhengzhou	31.28687999	Taizhou	28.95252936	Fuzhou	28.35105521
37	Xi'an	31.20168774	Hefei	28.82602387	Yangzhou	28.2251352
38	Fuzhou	31.171155	Karamay	28.80974567	Xuzhou	28.22382807
39	Guyuan	31.04495525	Weihai	28.68696002	Weihai	28.09827432
40	Wuhu	30.92593133	Xuzhou	28.63639201	Xi'an	27.95304416
41	Wenzhou	30.71392584	Tongren	28.58787611	Dalian	27.89023003
42	Hohhot	30.59931814	Lhasa	28.55710962	Quanzhou	27.72925379
43	Huzhou	30.5992593	Wuhu	28.39408061	Huzhou	27.63040428
44	Jieyang	30.50663472	Putian	28.39335155	Putian	27.58843284
45	Lishui	30.42234567	Dongying	28.34868026	Karamay	27.57486092
46	Chongqing	30.41349611	Suqian	28.28394755	Yantai	27.50297201
47	Zhaoqing	30.32940271	Zhengzhou	28.23117958	Zhengzhou	27.49373394
48	Weifang	30.32406868	Mianyang	28.13661108	Chongqing	27.4711332
49	Zibo	30.30157286	Quanzhou	28.13049629	Linyi	27.20253742
50	Taizhou	30.27860962	Lishui	28.01207448	Zibo	27.13701961
51	Weihai	30.21940261	Kunming	27.82906342	Taiyuan	27.04264455
52	Yangzhou	30.15342397	Chongqing	27.69134409	Binzhou	26.93876656
53	Urumchi	30.09624475	Taizhou	27.67208848	Lanzhou	26.92033056
54	Yantai	30.08174829	Haikou	27.43255983	Zhoushan	26.89781269
55	Haikou	30.03975159	Quzhou	27.36956189	Mianyang	26.89312738
56	Meizhou	29.94064762	Shijiazhuang	27.34935081	Ji'ning	26.76902705
57	Lianyungang	29.92950552	Huai'an	27.22975905	Nanchang	26.61301134
58	Taizhou	29.88451292	Yancheng	27.15331402	Zunyi	26.51695552
59	Quanzhou	29.85850603	Taiyuan	27.1283297	Suqian	26.41274475
60	Yancheng	29.82334386	Tai'an	27.11332065	Taizhou	26.36312314
61	Bijie	29.72152547	Changchun	27.01102582	Lishui	26.32727563
62	Huai'an	29.71489435	Ankang	26.97144669	Hefei	26.26583772
63	Shijiazhuang	29.56467071	Linyi	26.93496245	Laiwu	26.2163574
64	Kunming	29.49062509	Binzhou	26.89013086	Huai'an	26.12763901
65	Putian	29.15694682	Shantou	26.80772709	Quzhou	26.09108706
66	Huizhou	29.42081795	Liaocheng	26.73322568	Lianyungang	25.97427718
67	Zhoushan	29.40307687	Laiwu	26.52143667	Langfang	25.91075754
68	Nanning	29.25074469	Yulin	26.51019339	Heze	25.89552688

Ranking	2013	Total Score	2014	Total Score	2015	Total Score
69	Changchun	29.08591347	Harbin	26.4773582	Maoming	25.81151145
70	Zunyi	29.03121256	Nanning	26.35719117	Liaocheng	25.80940424
71	Ankang	28.95382881	Jiangmen	26.32201538	Huai'an	25.80914229
72	Nanchang	28.92195227	Ji'ning	26.25298334	Sanming	25.732903
73	Ya'an	28.89445637	Dezhou	26.03463083	Shijiazhuang	25.68829294
74	Quzhou	28.88097173	Tanzhou	25.95670859	Dezhou	25.64447143
75	Sanming	28.85237543	Erdos	25.93473767	Shenyang	25.63240149
76	Lanzhou	28.79962695	Xuancheng	25.88484552	Sanya	25.62986795
77	Sanya	28.59929221	Maoming	25.84180435	Tanzhou	25.56466934
78	Longyan	28.58965489	Sanming	25.7936112	Urumchi	25.33769787
79	Jining	28.5788622	Zhoushan	25.66285341	Yancheng	25.31635201
80	Yulin	28.5697557	Anshun	25.64279511	Longyan	25.15533234
81	Bengbu	28.56101207	Xianyang	25.64070739	Jiayuguan	25.10412027
82	Baotou	28.50869742	Longyan	25.58728123	Ji'an	25.02778151
83	Ningde	28.50703112	Bengbu	25.56930961	Huizhou	24.98448622
84	Tongren	28.48727078	Daqing	25.47092031	Bijie	24.96136171
85	Linyi	28.39303872	Guigang	25.44972234	Luoyang	24.72504829
86	Guiyang	28.34428595	Ji'an	25.41638085	Chaozhou	24.70486133
87	Lijiang	28.32993177	Beihai	25.41177784	Changchun	24.68293739
88	Haozhou	28.30411733	Hohhot	25.35118594	Wuhu	24.65696855
89	Shantou	28.29459663	Zhanjiang	25.33479176	Rizhao	24.63906141
90	Heze	28.27359627	Ningde	25.29630495	Yingtan	24.61744466
91	Daqing	28.26215783	Shaoguan	25.27197836	Qinghuangdao	24.55047541
92	Chuzhou	28.24210006	Yangjiang	25.26997873	Zhaoqing	24.50268278
93	Yangjiang	28.226842	Guiyang	25.23365421	Handan	24.47376383
94	Chaozhou	28.14679822	Heze	25.20900293	Nanning	24.46786527
95	Zhangjiajie	28.14293616	Mudanjiang	25.20529361	Ningde	24.37844854
96	Tanzhou	28.12629447	Sanya	25.15029349	Shizuishan	24.2823073
97	Dezhou	28.06055697	Tongchuan	25.13755318	Harbin	24.22461828
98	Jiangmen	28.036954	Lanzhou	25.11764589	Jieyang	24.22413066
99	Langfang	28.028859	Jieyang	25.00010567	Yunfu	24.19778305
100	Laiwu	27.92509917	Xinxiang	24.93873882	Jiangmen	24.15555128
101	Anshun	27.91089001	Meizhou	24.87838331	Hohhot	24.14746825
102	Liaocheng	27.90141528	Zunyi	24.84898979	Guigang	24.06794011
103	Fuyang	27.88567731	Zhaoqing	24.82343755	Shaoguan	24.01896363

Ranking	2013	Total Score	2014	Total Score	2015	Total Score
104	Yunfu	27.8824362	Langfang	24.7976426	Liuzhou	23.98205069
105	Zhanjiang	27.78064693	Handan	24.76261735	Cangzhou	23.94980407
106	Tongling	27.73867839	Yulin	24.75910462	Yangjiang	23.91332436
107	Yingkou	27.71900448	Rizhao	24.73988534	Loudi	23.88416647
108	Harbin	27.67874709	Tongling	24.71838511	Daqing	23.86089522
109	Xianyang	27.59312741	Nanping	24.70753287	Bengbu	23.83512256
110	Wuzhou	27.50901021	Deyang	24.67448247	Pingdingshan	23.82908198
111	Beihai	27.50747563	Yingtan	24.66055549	Ganzhou	23.80227811
112	Mianyang	27.4720631	Tangshan	24.61229854	Panzhihua	23.76923292
113	Guigang	27.41842767	Luoyang	24.57597358	Zaozhuang	23.75419303
114	Jiujiang	27.40967848	Qingyuan	24.48302504	Zhanjiang	23.73340303
115	Ganzhou	27.36633047	Nanchang	24.45321861	Beihai	23.72357881
116	Mudanjiang	27.35835073	Fangchenggang	24.44786779	Jiujiang	23.69272519
117	Ma'anshan	27.33932039	Shanwei	24.40731232	Shanwei	23.6734042
118	Shanwei	27.32650326	Hanzhong	24.40392405	Xinxiang	23.67049697
119	Anqing	27.27241884	Shizuishan	24.22940173	Xuchang	23.55655752
120	Guang'an	27.22322892	Zhongwei	24.22890028	Qingyuan	23.5200023
121	Dingxi	27.17771057	Zhoukou	24.21955072	Yichun	23.38855322
122	Tonghua	27.14154544	Cangzhou	24.19424358	Xi'ning	23.35699328
123	Yinchuan	27.10043265	Yingkou	24.18447946	Meizhou	23.33550513
124	Handan	27.06262827	Zaozhuang	24.13212102	Xiangtan	23.28438299
125	Guilin	27.04503712	Xiangyang	24.07625743	Zhangjiajie	23.22935042
126	Nanping	27.044921	Zhangjiajie	24.05873209	Baiyin	23.19225149
127	Shaoguan	27.03701316	Xuchang	24.0512829	Puyang	23.16812709
128	Fangchenggang	26.9385611	Shenyang	24.00874101	Jiaozuo	23.15758995
129	Xiangyang	26.93015772	Guilin	23.98166995	Huangshi	23.11098283
130	Cangzhou	26.92509704	Xiangtan	23.95991418	Anshun	23.09506622
131	Rizhao	26.85721753	Hezhou	23.944071	Hengshui	23.06876305
132	Qinzhou	26.83484743	Kaifeng	23.93344333	Zhumadian	23.06413742
133	Shuozhou	26.79922427	Zhuzhou	23.91543376	Kaifeng	23.06175179
134	Zhuzhou	26.77055623	Chuzhou	23.90316587	Nanping	22.9877987
135	Weinan	26.77049738	Shangqiu	23.8929067	Zhongwei	22.96719966
136	Luzhou	26.75838512	Jiaozuo	23.88794735	Xingtai	22.95818331
137	Jinzhou	26.67702692	Changde	23.88563926	Tongling	22.95496554
138	Wuhai	26.64562692	Tonghua	23.85190795	Erdos	22.95332242

Ranking	2013	Total Score	2014	Total Score	2015	Total Score
139	Dazhou	26.60448474	Bijie	23.84652016	Shangrao	22.95081663
140	Xinyang	26.59331009	Ma'anshan	23.81812279	Xiangyang	22.93948496
141	Huangshan	26.58222391	Puyang	23.81739461	Xianyang	22.90130293
142	Jincheng	26.56377607	Jiuyang	23.80892539	Jinzhong	22.89570915
143	Zhumadian	26.5557201	Anyang	23.79045272	Qinzhou	22.87693959
144	Tianshui	26.55225248	Shuozhou	23.77409569	Anyang	22.84479624
145	Jinzhong	26.53294747	Baoji	23.77366331	Chifeng	22.81318311
146	Pingxiang	26.53153766	Zigong	23.76877331	Tangshan	22.76861141
147	Songyuan	26.51069625	Wuzhou	23.7675404	Jinchang	22.76590111
148	Maoming	26.50445193	Haozhou	23.76293848	Baoding	22.7351239
149	Hezhou	26.49792803	Pingdingshan	23.75411775	Deyang	22.71158472
150	Ji'an	26.48594383	Anqing	23.71760489	Yichang	22.62214931
151	Suzhou	26.47962748	Pingxiang	23.65088055	Hebi	22.62086779
152	Tongchuan	26.44809585	Shangrao	23.58333476	Jincheng	22.61321954
153	Bingzhou	26.44254281	Xinyang	23.56972495	Tongchuan	22.56321282
154	Shangluo	26.41563326	Yueyang	23.5669614	Chuzhou	22.50384413
155	Kaifeng	26.41306262	Liuzhou	23.53536958	Yueyang	22.49741855
156	Yibin	26.4042654	Yunfu	23.53101558	Pingxiang	22.49576572
157	Yichang	26.38985064	Yichun	23.52342062	Xinyang	22.47420406
158	Zigong	26.37703851	Ganzhou	23.47527446	Jinzhou	22.44350316
159	Xining	26.34391693	Zhumadian	23.47247159	Weinan	22.44204523
160	Luoyang	26.33630853	Chaozhou	23.40757755	Shuozhou	22.43758265
161	Chizhou	26.23897244	Xianning	23.3959851	Huanggang	22.42055674
162	Deyang	26.22747725	Xingtai	23.37631164	Shangqiu	22.40981963
163	Siping	26.22356866	Shiyan	23.37003984	Tianshui	22.34982848
164	Xinxiang	26.21892033	Weinan	23.36914415	Lhasa	22.34747445
165	Yingtan	26.21753599	Fuzhou	23.34668087	Baoji	22.31639455
166	Zhoukou	26.19942576	Liaoyang	23.34198344	Pingliang	22.27975519
167	Qingyuan	26.19236489	Zhangye	23.33412293	Mudanjiang	22.27806436
168	Xinzhou	26.15167554	Baotou	23.33248171	Ankang	22.2705044
169	Lhasa	26.10645734	Qingzhou	23.32135789	Baotou	22.26283267
170	Jiaozuo	26.09628444	Huanggang	23.29459374	Yulin	22.17223032
171	Baoji	26.09307729	Dandong	23.28992487	Jingzhou	22.16645614
172	Ziyang	26.0466819	Yichang	23.2427232	Nanyang	22.14836824
173	Qingyang	26.0158456	Urumqi	23.2171598	Guilin	22.05859642

Ranking	2013	Total Score	2014	Total Score	2015	Total Score
174	Yueyang	26.00888631	Chizhou	23.19212793	Hanzhong	21.99689961
175	Shangqiu	26.00606851	Kiamusze	23.19170456	Yongzhou	21.97372641
176	Hanzhong	25.99430728	Chongzuo	23.18865575	Xinyu	21.95516095
177	Tai'an	25.96541335	Hengshui	23.15211524	Hezhou	21.95510187
178	Luliang	25.91499347	Luohe	23.1411323	Luohe	21.94399851
179	Changzhi	25.91415024	Jincheng	23.13833151	Sanmenxia	21.91779934
180	Huaihua	25.89692172	Huangshan	23.07708105	Dandong	21.90108679
181	Meishan	25.8940795	Guang'an	23.07141201	Yangquan	21.86772942
182	Baiyin	25.8570427	Suizhou	23.07087751	Changde	21.86751133
183	Suihua	25.84580133	Ziyang	23.00798509	Anqing	21.79640009
184	Nanchong	25.79835537	Yibin	22.9495441	Shaoyang	21.71317478
185	Liupanshui	25.77928564	Yuncheng	22.94616517	Luzhou	21.70846525
186	Suizhou	25.77402492	Yan'an	22.88480111	Laibin	21.68780958
187	Sanmenxia	25.7639962	Huangshi	22.88064019	Fangchenggang	21.66198076
188	Liuzhou	25.73881536	Xinzhou	22.87353054	Yibin	21.66097858
189	Zaozhuang	25.72429196	Xinyu	22.86731058	Yan'an	21.6583935
190	Chongzuo	25.71225121	Xi'ning	22.86464268	Ezhou	21.64654568
191	Baise	25.68712095	Chenzhou	22.85841841	Fuzhou	21.64330263
192	Shaoyang	25.63725313	Meishan	22.83487493	Zhoukou	21.63346651
193	Huanggang	25.61618109	Jingzhou	22.8195782	Zhuzhou	21.6039363
194	Changde	25.61307513	Hebi	22.80890456	Hengyang	21.59706117
195	Xiangtan	25.59160936	Qinhuangdao	22.80420791	Shiyan	21.57694556
196	Xingtai	25.55955115	Jilin	22.75092014	Yingkou	21.57462026
197	Yongzhou	25.52743871	Fuyang	22.75036886	Hechi	21.57314394
198	Guangyuan	25.50508156	Luzhou	22.73289503	Datong	21.54232324
199	Liaoyang	25.47506625	Sanmenxia	22.73258061	Ma'anshan	21.5076067
200	Laibin	25.28632905	Nanyang	22.68815464	Wuzhou	21.47297535
201	Longnan	25.23074141	Loudi	22.68082916	Chongzuo	21.4306154
202	Zhangye	25.22562647	Lianyungang	22.59914961	Chenzhou	21.42704914
203	Hengshui	25.1670701	Liupanshui	22.59387193	Tongren	21.42429288
204	Xianning	25.16658179	Wuhai	22.57417132	Tonghua	21.420923
205	Chenzhou	25.14843783	Baoding	22.57301177	Dingxi	21.40101962
206	Wuwei	25.12715143	Shaoyang	22.55522958	Xuancheng	21.39824716
207	Jiayuguan	25.07675257	Lijiang	22.5210159	Jilin	21.36894241
208	Hengyang	25.07649019	Yongzhou	22.49047917	Tsitsihar	21.36659157

Ranking	2013	Total Score	2014	Total Score	2015	Total Score
209	Yichun	25.04798726	Panzhihua	22.44932838	Jingdezhen	21.34767399
210	Zhongwei	25.00820683	Shangluo	22.43187121	Huaibei	21.34100964
211	Lincang	25.00528481	Jiuquan	22.41204787	Huludao	21.3188439
212	Shangrao	24.99568462	Guangyuan	22.40313415	Wuhai	21.26752664
213	Jilin	24.99244912	Jinchang	22.39977266	Xianning	21.26380454
214	Yuxi	24.96637874	Datong	22.36950199	Panjin	21.26281166
215	Nanyang	24.96379578	Suining	22.34133467	Suizhou	21.22423771
216	Yiyang	24.9571229	Huizhou	22.33917271	Jiuquan	21.18444717
217	Xinyu	24.93449086	Laibin	22.3326044	Yuncheng	21.1708109
218	Kiamusze	24.90928546	Baoshan	22.29140915	Guyuan	21.14898387
219	Huangshi	24.8622749	Huludao	22.2847517	Xiaogan	21.14284343
220	Liaoyuan	24.85238694	Benxi	22.23121146	Wuzhong	21.02759345
221	Baoding	24.8169996	Ezhou	22.2155822	Changzhi	21.00295737
222	Luohe	24.78024568	Hengyang	22.18171533	Shangluo	21.00008129
223	Dandong	24.77913617	Jinzhou	22.1744057	Yiyang	20.93584675
224	Puyang	24.76788599	Baiyin	22.16577955	Luliang	20.87949005
225	Yangquan	24.74957083	Yangquan	22.15698443	Chizhou	20.822936
226	Yuncheng	24.72384538	Tieling	22.10249663	Xinzhou	20.80540506
227	Zhaotong	24.69187018	Liu'an	22.09276539	Fuxin	20.78565171
228	Qinhuangdao	24.68899174	Anshan	22.06988363	Yinchuan	20.76281889
229	Tongliao	24.6646351	Suihua	22.0411031	Ulanqab	20.67643348
230	Chifeng	24.6230811	Tianshui	21.99842747	Dazhou	20.61457977
231	Xuancheng	24.59165152	Neijiang	21.99006953	Baise	20.60600428
232	Neijiang	24.54017665	Leshan	21.9670044	Benxi	20.57834246
233	Yan'an	24.53548755	Yiyang	21.96239791	Bazhong	20.53467525
234	Anshan	24.49421588	Chifeng	21.9398311	Heihe	20.52026111
235	Xiaogan	24.48810664	Xiaogan	21.92333861	Qujin	20.50229655
236	Huaibei	24.48491798	Jiayuguan	21.91209005	Huangshan	20.4975428
237	Jiuquan	24.41982121	Chengde	21.79638687	Guangyuan	20.48871345
238	Huainan	24.4091366	Panjin	21.78820858	Liaoyang	20.48084724
239	Jixi	24.33164265	Changzhi	21.75607555	Neijiang	20.4808428
240	Pingdingshan	24.29129062	Huaihua	21.75156023	Suzhou	20.47869081
241	Baoshan	24.20565774	Heihe	21.74730039	Zigong	20.41742291
242	Xuchang	24.20343055	Tsitsihar	21.70717505	Zhangjiakou	20.41275276
243	Pingliang	24.17851592	Songyuan	21.62473651	Huaihua	20.36528015

Ranking	2013	Total Score	2014	Total Score	2015	Total Score
244	Hulun Buir	24.16629174	Qingyang	21.6246461	Liupanshui	20.34208337
245	Loudi	24.13940262	Liaoyuan	21.61387102	Guangyuan	20.30363965
246	Jingdezhen	24.12349718	Jingzhou	21.5497441	Linfen	20.28710064
247	Ezhou	24.02221437	Dingxi	21.53214176	Huainan	20.27789857
248	Chaoyang	24.01804028	Guyuan	21.48375843	Tieling	20.26416528
249	Hebi	23.98819322	Suzhou	21.45618899	Meishan	20.24009109
250	Wuzhong	23.85840931	Ya'an	21.44901256	Songyuan	20.22630385
251	Fuxin	23.83916915	Luliang	21.44675982	Fuzhou	20.212493
252	Anyang	23.81418164	Huaibei	21.43263162	Kiamusze	20.19061133
253	Shiyan	23.74315924	Huainan	21.39409254	Siping	20.18384272
254	Qujing	23.73275226	Fuxin	21.37835418	Heyuan	20.12601413
255	Bazhong	23.70083565	Hechi	21.35527794	Chengde	20.09226741
256	Panzhihua	23.6912813	Yuxi	21.24154052	Liu'an	20.00438432
257	Simao	23.65792822	Chaoyang	21.23931555	Haozhou	19.97697497
258	Liuan	23.65610125	Baise	21.04735839	Fuyang	19.97162271
259	Datong	23.59334984	Zhangjiakou	20.99162466	Qingyang	19.87621834
260	Zhangjiakou	23.56903159	Bazhong	20.92438752	Ya'an	19.87357287
261	Linfen	23.53605198	Jinzhong	20.86385155	Anshan	19.86874399
262	Leshan	23.41390011	Simao	20.83509843	Yuxi	19.83053621
263	Tieling	23.40070586	Linfen	20.8213496	Baoshan	19.8256821
264	Tangshan	23.33095861	Nanchong	20.8170299	Chaoyang	19.78569041
265	Heihe	23.14786843	Heyuan	20.77084895	Jingzhou	19.69693629
266	Jingzhou	23.06648666	Baicheng	20.76170862	Lijiang	19.66573163
267	Huludao	22.88579717	Tongliao	20.65168075	Leshan	19.31692968
268	Baishan	22.72421096	Pingliang	20.55053453	Shuangyashan	19.27169571
269	Baicheng	22.70695706	Qujing	20.44273709	Liaoyuan	19.26286049
270	Fuzhou	22.54629942	Zhaotong	20.31739326	Jixi	19.21824461
271	Jinchang	22.52260689	Fushun	20.30098629	Longnan	19.19845534
272	Tsitsihar	22.39315561	Wuwei	20.18347778	Nanchong	18.90797313
273	Chengde	22.29916991	Wuzhong	20.08448098	Ziyang	18.82360387
274	Benxi	22.27807174	Lincang	19.98745836	Lincang	18.74371446
275	Hegang	22.26184608	Baishan	19.97884912	Qitaihe	18.70256251
276	Jingzhou	22.14427132	Longnan	19.80620174	Baishan	18.66820494
277	Shizuishan	21.97630984	Hegang	19.76069487	Hulun Buir	18.64460567
278	Heyuan	21.97302556	Hulun Buir	19.72977459	Suihua	18.60348217

Ranking	2013	Total Score	2014	Total Score	2015	Total Score
279	Fushun	21.90451756	Jixi	19.62496578	Baicheng	18.48716658
280	Shuangyashan	21.875706	Dazhou	19.42109109	Bayannur	18.46868154
281	Ulanqab	21.50893554	Siping	19.40750194	Tongliao	18.38412108
282	Hechi	21.32569269	Ulanqab	19.14033394	Hegang	18.09134698
283	Panjin	21.14079525	Yinchuan	19.10361843	Simao	18.04680987
284	Suining	20.78870782	Yichun	18.89969462	Sui'ning	17.69973378
285	Karamay	20.75800235	Bayannur	18.52832263	Wuwei	17.57176746
286	Qitaihe	20.45542804	Shuangyashan	18.29283472	Zhangye	16.5658101
287	Bayannur	20.40408748	Qitaihe	18.22831856	Zhaotong	16.30021263
288	Yichun	18.68479847	Jingdezhen	17.4843753	Yichun	14.55580564
289	Sansha	8.431096979	Sansha	7.156975416	Sansha	8.530835314

Endnotes

1 Gérard Roland, *Transformation and Economics*, translated by Zhang Fan. Beijing: Peking University Press, 2002, pp. 5–11.

2 F. L. Wu, 'The post-socialist entrepreneurial city as a state project: Shanghai's regionalization in question', *Urban Studies*, issue 9, 2003, 1673–1698.

3 Li Xuexin, Tian Guangzeng, and Miao Changhong, 'Economic transformation of regional central cities: Mechanism and mode', *Research on Urban Development*, Vol. 17, issue 4, 2010, pp. 26–32.

4 H. K. Hansen and L. Winther, 'The spaces of urban economic geographies: Industrial transformation in the outer city of Copenhagen', *Danish Journal of Geography*, Vol. 107, issue 2, 2007, pp. 45–58.

5 Li Hanlin, 'Ten theoretical frontier problems of study on resource-based urban economic restructuring', *Gansu Theory Journal*, issue 1, 2005, pp. 53–56.

6 Kiril Stanilov, *The Post-socialist City: Urban Form and Space Transformations in Central and Eastern Europe after Socialism*, Cincinnati: GeoJournal Library, 2007, pp. 347–359.

7 Martin Seeleib-Kaiser, 'A dual transformation of the German welfare state', *West European Politics*, Vol. 25, issue 4, 2002, pp. 25–48.

8 Henning Nuissl and Dieter Rink, *Urban Sprawl and Post-socialist Transformation: The Case of Leipzig (Germany)*, Leipzig: UFZ-Bericht, 2003, pp. 28–30.

9 Franco Bianchini, 'Remaking European cities: The role of cultural policies' in *Cultural Policy and Urban Regeneration*, eds F. Bianchini and M. Parkinson, Manchester: Manchester University Press, 1993, pp. 1–20.

10 GLA Economics, *London's Creative Sector: 2004 Update*, London: Greater London Authority, 2004.

11 H. K. Lysgard and O. Tveiten, 'Cultural economy at work in the city of Kristiansand: Cultural policy as incentive for urban innovation', *AI & Society*, Vol. 19, issue 4, 2005, pp. 485–499.

12 Andy C. Pratt, 'Creative cities: The cultural industries and the creative class', *Human Geography*, Vol. 20, issue 2, 2008, pp. 107–117.

13 Zhu Bin, 'Experience of the adjustment of industrial structure and urban transformation in the United States of America', *Science and Technology Industry Parks*, issue 8, 2007, pp. 92–95.

14 Zhong Jie Wu, Wang Jing, and Sang Jinyan, 'Industrial transformation of resource-based city of our country from the perspective of low-carbon economy' in *Dongyue Symposium*, 2010.

15 Zhao Hong, 'Headquarters economy to boost the city's economic transition', *Taiyuan Science and Technology*, issue 6, 2007, pp. 13–11.

16 Xu Jiansheng and Liu Huihui, 'The path choice of transformation from the traditional manufacturing city to the knowledge city', *Urban Insight*, issue 1, 2010, pp. 154–161.

17 Victorian Government, *Department of Planning and Development: Melbourne Metropolitan Strategy*, Melbourne: Victorian Government, 1994.

18 Wu Zhijie and Zhang Lili, 'Circular economy – Sustainable economic development model', *Journal of Ecology*, Vol. 25, issue 10, 2006, pp. 1,245–1,251.

19 Dong Suocheng, Li Zehong, Li Bin et al., 'Economic transformation and strategic exploration of China's resource-based cities', *China Population Resources and Environment*, Vol. 17, issue 5, 2007, pp. 17–12.

20 Da Liangjun, Tian Zhihui, and Chen Xiaoshuang, 'Eco city development and construction model', *Modern Urban Research*, issue 7, 2009, pp. 11–17.

21 Zhu Mingfeng, Hong Tianqiu, and Ye Qiang, 'Sustainable development indicator system of resource-based cities based on neural network', *Journal of University of Science & Technology China*, issue 6, 2005.

22 Zang Shuying, Zhi Ruizhi, and Sun Xuemeng, 'Quantitative assessment of sustainable development of resource-based cities based on the ecological footprint model – Taking Daqing as an example', *Geographical Science*, issue 8, 2006.

23 Wang Fei, *Indicator System Construction and Comprehensive Evaluation Research on Resource based Cities Sustainable Development*, Daqing Petroleum Universitys Master's thesis, March 2006.

24 Wei Lihua, Lu Ming, and Yan Xiao Pei, 'The meaning, definition and research framework of "Transformation Cities" during social and economic transition period of China', *Modern Urban Research*, issue 9, 2006.

25 Zhu Tiezhen, 'Urban transformation and innovation', *City*, issue 6, 2006.

26 Ye Yumin and Tang Jie, 'Research on the development of urban industrial development in Shenzhen', *City and Regional Planning Research*, issue 1, 2011.

27 Chai Yanwei and Zhang Chun, 'Urban units from the perspective of geography: The key to the transformation of Chinese cities', *International Urban Planning*, issue 5, 2009.

28 Li Yanjun, *Theoretical Framework and Support System of Urban Transformation in China*, China Building Industry Press, 2011, pp. 1–40.

29 Wei Houkai, 'The study of urban and regional planning in China's urban transformation strategy', *City and Regional Planning Research*, issue 1, 2011.

30 Wu Fulong, *Transformation and Reconstruction: A Multidimensional Perspective of Chinese Urban Development*, Nanjing: Southeast University Press, 2007, pp. 2–8.

31 John R. Logan, *The New Chinese City: Globalization and Market Reform*, Hoboken, NJ: Wiley-Blackwell, 2002, pp. xv–xvi.

32 Lin Yifu, 'Introspection on viability, the economic transformation and the new classical economics', *Economic Research*, issue 12, 2002.

33 Li Qingchun, 'The developing strategy of central regions in China based on the regional viability', *Special Economic Zone*, issue 2, 2007.

34 Wang Ke, 'The development and cultivation of self-development ability in poor areas of China – Based on the new perspective of the main functional area', *Gansu Social Science*, issue 8, 2008.

35 Cen Jie, Wu Zhonggui, and Han Yu, 'Research on the promotion of entrepreneurial economy and regional viability – Based on perspective of the integration of regional elements', *Hubei Social Science*, issue 5, 2009.

36 Michael E. Porter, *Competitive Advantage of Nations: Creating and Sustaining Superior Performance*, New York: Simon & Schuster, 2011.

37 Mao Jiangxing, He Yijian. Study on the life cycle model of resource-based cities, Geography and Geo-Information Science, 2008(01):56-60.

38 Chen Yuanzhi and Shang Zhitian, *How to solve the problem of 'best game no one played' in promoting the PPP model?* Leadership reference (CELAP), 2006.

SHANGHAI: A VISION OF A NEW GLOBAL CITY

7

In the first half of the 20th century, Shanghai was dynamic and international, far ahead of many other Chinese cities. Although Shanghai did not see the same immediate rapid development of the Pearl River Delta region after opening-up began in 1978, from the late 1980s it recaptured its role as China's gateway to the world and the world's entry point to China. This was the focus of Shanghai's World Fair Expo 2010. In 2016, Mayor Yang Xiong proclaimed that Shanghai would become 'a global city of excellence' by 2040 and placed this at the heart of his vision. Shanghai aspires to be considered in the same category as London and New York, and while it is yet to become as international as those cities, its economy and infrastructure already promise that it will emulate and surpass its golden interwar period and become once again one of the world's great cities.

An Overview of Shanghai

Shanghai is one of the four directly controlled municipalities of the PRC–equivalent to a province. It aspires to be a global financial centre by 2020, as directed by the State Council, and is already a transport hub, with the world's busiest container port. Located on the Yangtze River Delta in Eastern China, Shanghai sits on the south edge of the mouth of the Yangtze, emptying its waters into the Eastern China Sea. It has a land area of 6340.5 km^2 (2013). Shanghai city proper is bisected by the Huangpu River: Puxi (浦西), on the west side, is

the historic centre of the city, and includes the districts of Yangpu (杨浦), Hongkou (虹口), Putuo (普陀), Changning (长宁), Xuhui (徐汇), Jing'an (静安), and Huangpu (黄浦). Pudong (浦东新区) is located on the east side and is the location of Shanghai's rapid development, including its now famous skyline and the Lujiazui financial district. The outer districts, or suburbs, surround the city proper, including Baoshan (宝山), Minhang (闵行), Jiading (嘉定), Jinshan (金山), Songjiang (松江), Qingpu (青浦), Fengxian (奉贤), and the rural eastern part of Pudong. Chongming (崇明) lies in the north of the Shanghai Peninsula on three inhabited islands in the Yangtze estuary: Chongming (崇明岛), Changxing (长兴岛), and Hengsha (横沙岛). From 2012 to 2014, Shanghai took the third position in the ranking list of China's Urban Transformation and Upgrading Capability for three consecutive years.

According to the Shanghai Master Plan (2016–40), the policy target for Shanghai is that it becomes a global city: a key participant in the economy of the 21st century, and a cosmopolitan centre for innovation, humanity, and ecology.[1] According to the plan, the city's population will be limited to 25 million by 2040. The total land area allocated for construction will be limited to 3,200 km^2, 26 per cent of which will be residential, according to the plan. Forests and parks will occupy the rest of the city's land to make it ecologically friendly. Forest coverage will reach 25 per cent, and each resident will have 15 m² of public parks or green land on average by 2040. Average density of PM2.5 – hazardous fine particle air pollution – will be reduced to about 20 µg per cubic metre. By 2040 more than half of downtown residents will rely on public transport, and over 60 per cent of residents will have a subway station within 600 m of their homes.

The aim to make Shanghai a global city is in a sense a return to the past to make a new future. In the 1920s and the early 1930s, Shanghai was one of the world's most vibrant, dynamic, and cosmopolitan cities, the 'Pearl of the Orient'. This ended with Japanese invasion in 1937 and the turmoil and carnage of the Second World War.

Historically, Shanghai was also a migrant city, attracting a large international population as well as a significant influx of Chinese drawn to economic, social, and cultural opportunities.

The new Shanghai must also draw on this international and domestic resource if it is truly to become a global city. At the end of 2013, the city's resident population was 24,151,500. Of this, the permanent resident population was 14,251,400 while the number of its non-native permanent, or floating, population was 9,900,100.

Shanghai is a popular tourist destination renowned for its historical landmarks such as the Bund, City God Temple, and Yu Garden as well as the Lujiazui skyline and major museums including the Shanghai Museum and China Art Museum. In 2013, Shanghai greeted 7,574,000 international tourists; international tourism foreign exchange income was US$53.37 billion. The city received 275,000,000 domestic tourists, and domestic tourism revenue was CNY340 billion. 25 per cent of China's non-Chinese international residents live in Shanghai, but this figure is still only 170,000.

Figure 7.1: Night View of Lujiazui, Shanghai

Although a province in its own right, Shanghai's development as a global city, or more precisely as a global city region, is linked to the integrated development of the Yangtze River Delta, which takes in part of the key provinces of Jiangsu and Zhejiang. It is facilitated by the transportation hub in the new Hongqiao Business District with rapid rail links to cities such as Suzhou, Wuxi, Hangzhou, and Nanjing. While the new transport hub links Shanghai with its immediate hinterland, the new deepwater port opens Shanghai to the world. The city will form the Chinese character 水 ('water') – in its spatial pattern of regional development.

While Shanghai covers only 0.065 per cent of China's land area, its economy constitutes 3.8 per cent of national GDP, its port carries 17.8 per cent of all container traffic, and its customs facilities deal with 19.5 per cent of all imports and exports. The Yangtze River Delta region – Jiangsu Province, Zhejiang Province, and the city of Shanghai, are connected. They have similar cultural backgrounds, economic integration, and social connections. The Yangtze River Delta covers 2.2 per cent of the country's land area and 10.4 per cent of the whole population, creates 22.1 per cent of the country's GDP, 24.5 per cent of fiscal revenue, and 28.5 per cent of total import and export volume. It has become one of the most developed areas of China's economy, science and technology, and culture.

Since 1949, Shanghai has experienced at least three major transformations. The first transition began with the founding of modern China and was essentially domestic. In the 1930s, Shanghai was an international financial centre, a major trade centre in the Far East, and the most important industrial and commercial city in China. After 1949, Shanghai's development was determined by the needs of the new state. Shanghai had a major

Figure 7.2: Shanghai Yangshan Deepwater Port

responsibility for the revitalisation of the national economy and especially its industrial base. Shanghai had the best equipment, was the most productive, and was technologically advanced. At the time of the first Five-Year Plan (1953–57), one third of the country's cotton yarn, cotton, cigarettes, and more than half of the medicines and daily necessities were provided by Shanghai.

The second transition from the late 1980s began the internationalisation of Shanghai. This was signalled by the fundamental change from a planned to a market economy. Nevertheless, the 1980s was a difficult period for Shanghai, since while the opening-up and reform began in south Guangdong, the old model persisted in Shanghai. Although Shanghai's economic growth rate increased for ten consecutive years between 1982 and 1991 it was still lower than the national average. In this period, Shanghai's GDP grew from CNY60,000 million to CNY80,000 million.

But Shanghai's administration could control only a small part of this – only CNY5 to 6 billion every year, a problem that persists for all China's cities. Shanghai's future changed in 1990 when the Party Central Committee announced the development and opening of Pudong. In 1992, the Fourteenth Party Congress report proposed to build Shanghai into an international economic, financial, and trade centre as soon as possible, to rejuvenate the Yangtze River Delta and the Yangtze River Basin. The new direction for Shanghai was properly set in motion. Shanghai was put forward for the '321' industrial development policy, to put service industry into a more prominent position, and to restructure the role and location of industry – particularly heavy industry – by moving away from the centre. The new development of Pudong was to play a major role in this shift alongside the establishment of four industrial bases in the northern, southern, eastern, and western suburbs. Simultaneously, a policy of encouraging foreign capital and enterprise – multinational and high-tech – right across the municipality was declared on favourable terms, including low land rent, for the incoming companies. In the next period (1992–2007), Shanghai had 16 consecutive years of two-digit growth. The average GDP growth rate of 12.7 per cent exceeded the national equivalent by two percentage points.

The most recent transformation began in 2008 following the international financial crisis. In the short term, this constituted a blow to Shanghai's export-driven economy, but the crisis was the catalyst for a fundamental shift in the balance of the global economy, potentially to the advantage of Shanghai. In the first instance, Shanghai's economy suffered more than the country as a whole and the growth rate fell below the national average. Shanghai, nevertheless, had a historic opportunity on the global stage, but only if it faced up to some fundamental challenges. The impact of the international financial crisis made not only Shanghai but also China more significant in the global economy while highlighting Shanghai's deep-seated structural contradictions. Shanghai was too dependent on land finance, had a legacy of a lack of financial control, large-scale investment, and an export-driven development model. At the same time, the crisis was an opportunity and an incentive for a radical transformation.

Challenges and Bottlenecks for a Global Shanghai

The old model became a major obstacle to Shanghai's economic development. Shanghai could not continue to rely on incoming investment stimulated through low land rents, nor on the export of commodities, which suffered a drastic decline in the post-2008 environment.

Economic Development

A difficult problem for Shanghai is that the slowdown of the export market and the planned diffusion of heavy industry to the suburbs has been faster than the introduction of high-tech manufacturing and high-end service industries. The very structure of the old model, conducive to a traditional industrial base, inhibits the emergence of such a radically different environment. High-end service industries such as finance, logistics, culture, information, and the siting of headquarters are shackled by the existing system of tax, regulation, credit, and other legal restrictions. The incentives and mechanisms for innovation need to be improved. In addition, high-end service suffers from the imperfection of market mechanisms in which labour, land, and capital elements are segmented, leading to price distortion and a lack of cohesion in the system.

Spatial Layout

Shanghai's urban planners have looked around the world and drawn the conclusion that urban spatial structure is one of the important factors affecting the efficiency and competitiveness of cities. Since the 1980s, due to the wide use of network technology, information technology, and modern communication technology, space in major international conurbations developed 'multi centres'. In London, the coexistence of the City and Canary Wharf is a good example of this. The centre of Shanghai still has a more traditional, even European, feel. While this may prove to be an advantage in attracting an international population, this is outweighed by the lack of not only 'spatial carrier support' for the suburbs but also a wide range of other social and cultural amenities. At the moment, the suburbs are not acting as nodes of urban function for the new city. As a result, the urbanisation of the city falls short of international levels.

Public Service

The economic advance of Shanghai has not been matched by its social and cultural development. For long-term success Shanghai has to become more liveable not only for the long-term international residents but also for its existing population.

The development of public services in education, health, culture, and other areas seriously lags behind economic development. There is a huge gap between social and public cultural service supply and demand. Moreover, this imbalance is highlighted in the suburbs, which are disadvantaged in terms of social and cultural resources. The gap in education, culture, health, and other social allocation of resources between the urban and rural areas continues to increase. Finally, an ageing population further aggravates the imbalance in the allocation of social resources. An inadequate labour supply increases pressure on the balance of social security funds, pension services, medical services, community services, and other resources.

Shanghai's government is concerned that its migrant population places an additional strain on its social provision. Yet this very population would also counterbalance the impact of an ageing population, for which Shanghai is about 20 years ahead of the rest of China.

Measures for the Transformation and Development of Shanghai

The Shanghai Municipality implements a strategic 'innovation drive, transition and development' to shape the new Shanghai. These subheading are the strategic policy rubric.

Three Absolute Don'ts:

- Don't act at the expense of the environment and waste resources.

- Don't accumulate social contradictions.

- Don't increase the debt to future generations.

Economic development should be based on reducing:

Four Dependences:

- Reducing dependence on the heavy chemical industries.

- Reducing dependence on real estate.

- Reducing dependence on labour-intensive processing industry.

- Reducing dependence on investment pull.

The negatives would then be replaced by positives:

Six Innovations and Six Transitions:

- Innovation for the service development environment.

- Accelerating the transition to a service economy.

- Innovation for the high-tech industry environment.

- Accelerating the transition to an innovation economy.

- Innovation to expand domestic demand.

- Accelerating transition to the inward pull.

- Innovation for energy saving.

- Speeding up a transition to a green economy.

- Innovation in the mechanism of urban and rural development.

- Accelerating the integration of urban and rural areas.

- Innovation in the social livelihood system of the people.

- Accelerating transition of sharing development.

All the above constitute a fundamental change in the conception of how Shanghai not only maintains its success in economic growth but also

Redevelopment of Yangpu District

Yangpu District is located in the northeastern part of downtown Shanghai. It hosts one-third of Shanghai's universities including the prestigious Fudan University. These universities have existed for approximately a century. Yangpu District was the birthplace of China's modern industry over a century ago. Yangpu District saw the first power and water plants in China. These developments have won Yangpu District a reputation as a 'Three One-century District'. Yangpu Knowledge/Creative Zone – based around the educational hubs of Fudan and Tongji and regeneration of old industrial warehouses – is regarded as equivalent to East London. The district has made itself prominent in technological innovation thanks to the following efforts.

First, for the purpose of industry–university–research integration, the local government has endeavoured to promote the profound connection between universities, communities, and high-tech zones. Colleges, universities, and research institutes are encouraged to share facilities and resources.

Second, the local government has made efforts to attract innovation resources from both home and abroad by promoting high technology transfer and innovation resource allocation centres. Yangpu District has maintained regular communication with the San Francisco Bay Area Committee, exchanging ideas and technologies. It has built the National Technology Transfer and Trading Centre.

Third, the local government has improved the service system for entrepreneurship and innovation. It provides comfortable offices for big companies and joint office space for SMEs. Yangpu District provides customised housing solutions or house-renting subsidies for talented personnel. It offers high-end internationalised living communities that can meet the needs of high-end personnel such as executives from multinational companies.

grows into a new position in the global division of labour. This would alleviate long-term pressure on land, other resources, and the environment. The new focus is on technology intensive industries with an emphasis on science, the information and knowledge economy, and the creative industries. In June 2015, Shanghai announced the 22 items on accelerating the construction of a global centre for science and innovation. The core concept is to solve the tough problems which hinder innovation.

Renewed emphasis will be placed on the service sector as an important symbol of economic growth and modernisation, in order to make Shanghai part of the global service industry. During the 'Twelfth Five-Year' period (2011–15), Shanghai's per capita GDP exceeded $10,000, and as the engine of this economic growth service elements had become more important than manufacturing.

Most crucially, the city is now located at a tipping point between a key domestic economic centre and a global city. Traditional international economic centres, such as London and New York, and other metropolises, are interconnected in a global financial and value chain network. A global city, such as London, is not only a general economic centre, but also a centralised control point in the world economy. It is a major hub, and gathering place, for financial institutions and professional services companies, high-tech industry R&D and a production base for new ideas and products. In a period of global economic transition post-2008, Shanghai has the designated role of becoming a key participant in a new global economic division of labour.

The World Expo 2010 Shanghai China was held on both banks of the Huangpu River from 1 May to

31 October 2010. The theme of the exposition was 'Better City – Better Life' and signifies Shanghai's new status in the 21st century as the 'next great world city'. Shanghai is at the centre of the most dynamic economic region of the world, on the coast of East Asia. With the establishment of the ASEAN Free Trade Area, the Closer Economic Partnership Arrangement (CEPA), and the

World Expo 2010 Shanghai China – Showing Shanghai to the World

A key moment in Shanghai's transition to world city was Expo 2010, explicitly designed not only to stimulate the infrastructural development of the city and its internationalisation, but also to provide a legacy of expertise and resources, such as:

- land, venues, facilities and assets;

- a new city brand;

- better-trained personnel with operational experience;

- new soft assets to correspond to the city's hardware;

- international professional talents, international business organisations, greater international competitiveness, and a new urban management mechanism.

All these are aimed at making and keeping Shanghai the 'the international window' of China.

Figure 7.5: China Pavilion at Shanghai World Expo

implementation of cross-strait 'three links', East Asian cities will have an enhanced population, logistics, technology, information, and capital flows. All of this will speed up Shanghai's city grade crossing, accelerating its transformation to an intercontinental and international economic centre. This is a historic opportunity for Shanghai.

The economic initiatives of Shanghai enhance the city's social development – its 'liveability' for international residents and existing citizens. The aim is to transform Shanghai from a 'moderately well-off' to a 'harmonious' society.

Shanghai has now reached the level of a middle-income developed economy. In the past, the service sector has been constrained by the comparatively low purchasing power of Shanghai compared with western cities. Chinese citizens felt limited as consumers because of the need to save to cover health, education, and other social provision. Improving social provision, along with a technological and cultural upgrade, is therefore a key priority. Nevertheless, despite these difficulties the residents' consumption capability has been markedly enhanced and high-grade consumer goods are now more accessible and cheaper. Citizens now expect better quality of life and this may find an expression in the willingness and capacity of citizen public participation in urban governance. The old adage of 'stressing economy, neglecting society' no longer works.

Shanghai's development must be seen in the context of the wider integrated Yangtze River Delta region. There is a daily surge of population flow in the Yangtze River Delta alongside capital, personnel, information, goods, and business flows. This not only promotes the real-estate market and integrates the labour market, but also reshapes the boundaries for administrative policy, leading to social insurance service across the region.

Shanghai: A Vision of a New Global City

79

Figure 7.6: Shanghai Hongqiao Transportation Hub

Improving Urban Governance Structure

Shanghai has accelerated the transition from administrative government to service government by forming a new governance structure. In 2015, the city began to reform the street management system. Street management responsibility for social issues was increased while responsibility for economic issues was decreased. By increasing social management functions and ceasing to develop economy at the street level, Shanghai improves governance in the villages and strengthens the mechanism of villagers' self-government.

Weakening the Incentive System for Pursuit of GDP

Shanghai gave up the GDP-oriented assessment criteria of government officials. Instead, it stressed improving public services and strengthening social management. The new assessment system was trialled during the 12th Five-Year Plan period. This system has 42 indicators, covering transforming the development mode, improving innovation capability, systematic reform, and building a harmonious society. Of these indicators, 30 are relevant to innovation.

Propelling Systematic Reforms in the Pilot Free Trade Zone

The Pilot Free Trade Zone (FTZ), inaugurated in September 2013, aims to become a driving force for China's reform and opening-up. In April 2015, the FTZ expanded from 28 km² to 120 km² to better fulfil its mission, incorporating three more areas: Lujiazui Financial and Trade Zone, Jinqiao Development Zone, and Zhangjiang High-Tech Park. The FTZ covers several aspects. Approval requirements shall be replaced by registration, which will remove administrative burdens for foreign investors and will speed up the implementation process of projects in the FTZ. This is in contrast to the Foreign Investment Guidance Catalogue, thereby classifying industry sectors in China into the 'Encouraged', 'Restricted', and 'Permitted' categories, monitoring how foreigners may invest. A much simpler 'negative list' shall apply specifically to foreign investment in the FTZ and certain restricted industries shall be opened up to foreign investment within the FTZ.

Figure 7.7: China (Shanghai) Pilot Free Trade Zone

Endnotes

1   Shanghai Master Plan (2016–40), [EB/OL], http://www.supdri.com/2040/index. php?c=message&a=type&tid=31 (accessed 28 April 2018).

NANCHANG: TOWARDS A LOW-CARBON CITY

8

A dominant feature of China's urban development and an ongoing preoccupation for many outside observers is the high use of carbon-based energy sources. However, China is currently emphasising and developing much more efficient and low-carbon energy sources.

To be significant this must not only apply to high-profile cities such as Shanghai but also must become part of mainstream development. Nanchang, although much less well-known, is more representative of this stage of China's urban priorities both in terms of energy and the incorporation of the natural environment.

Nanchang has a compelling strategy for industrial transformation in the context of its distinctive topography and natural setting. It demonstrates that China's urban concerns are not limited to the most famous and fashionable centres.

Figure 8.1: Nanchang Bayi Bridge

An Overview of Nanchang

Nanchang is the capital city of Jiangxi Province in southeastern China, located in the mid-north of the province, downstream of the Gan and Fu Rivers. It is on the southwest shore of the biggest freshwater lake in China, Poyang Lake. In the northwest the city is hilly while to the southeast there are many lakes and a dense water network. The Nanchang Uprising of 1 August 1927 is recognised by the Communist Party as 'firing the first gunshot against Nationalists'. The city has been known as 'the City of Heroes', 'the birthplace of the People's Liberation Army' since 1949.

At the end of 2014, the city's resident population was 5,240,200, and the total GDP of Nanchang was CNY366.796 billion. From 2012 to 2014, Nanchang took, respectively, the seventy-second, one hundred and fifteenth, and fifty-seventh position in the ranking list of China's Urban Transformation and Upgrading Capability. The city covers an area of 7,402 km², 617 km² of which is urban area and 220 km² of which is built-up or urbanised area. The following counties, districts, and areas are under the jurisdiction of Nanchang Municipal Administration: Nanchang County (南昌县), Jinxian County (进贤县), Anyi County (安义县), Donghu District (东湖区), Xihu District (西湖区), Qingyunpu District (青云谱区), Qingshanhu District (青山湖区), Wanli District (湾里区), and Xinjian District (新建区), as well as Nanchang Economic and Technological Development Zone (南昌经济技术开发区), Nanchang High and New Technology Industry Development Zone (南昌高新技术开发区), and Honggutan New District (红谷滩新区). In 2016, Jiangxi Province officially released the Grand Nanchang Metropolitan Area Planning, whose space range includes the whole region of Nanchang and part of Fuzhou, Yichun, and Shangrao. According to the planning, Nanchang Metropolitan Area will include 23,000 km² with a permanent population of 14 million by 2030.

The Basis and Challenges of Nanchang's Transition to a Low-carbon City

In 2009, the First World Low Carbon and Ecological Economic Conference took place in Nanchang. The city's efforts to construct a low-carbon city were facilitated through extensive international cooperation with technical support from the United States, the United Kingdom, and Austria. In the same year, the National Development and Reform Commission (NDRC) selected Nanchang as one of the first pilot low-carbon cities.

The city has favourable conditions for constructing a low-carbon city due to the natural environment and its climate. Nanchang is located in a subtropical evergreen broad-leaved forest zone, with four distinct seasons and a mild climate. This natural environment greatly facilitates the forming and protection of a diversified ecology. Moreover, Nanchang lies near Poyang Lake, which provides abundant food for migrant birds to live and breed in the wetlands. This 'urban migrant birds' scenario is the environmental basis for the city's development.

Figure 8.2: Xiang Lake Wetland Park, Nanchang City

Figure 8.3: Ganjiang Riverside of Nanchang City

Nanchang: Towards a Low-carbon City

Rapid Economic Development

This is defined as 'economic improvement, rapid change and everyone striving for prosperity'.

A Foundation of Environmental Protection: 'Forest and Garden Nanchang'

In recent years, Nanchang has promoted a circular economy to improve resource-dependent industries. During the Eleventh Five-Year Plan, the unit power consumption fell by 20 per cent, and the discharging of major pollutants dropped, meeting the Plan's target. The urban sewage centralised processing rate reached 92 per cent and harmless treatment rate of household garbage attained 100 per cent.

Now energy-saving design and energy auditing has been applied comprehensively in new building construction projects together with the application of reusable energy.

Figure 8.4: Pavilion of Prince Teng in Nanchang City

The Challenges for Nanchang:

Unbalanced Industrial Structure of Nanchang

The industrial layout of Nanchang concentrates on low-end manufacturing industry with low resource utilisation rate. The proportion of high-quality products, high-tech products, and high added-value products is still low. Most enterprises are small and medium. It lags behind coastal areas, where there are many large enterprises of high efficiency and advanced management. Nanchang is also facing new problems of industry transfer. Many enterprises with potential environmental issues are keen to relocate to Nanchang from coastal areas, and this will bring further problems.

Nanchang's improvement in these areas is still insufficient to keep up with economic development and population growth. It is short of investment in transportation, water supply, drainage systems, and hazardous waste treatment facilities. The tension between rapid urban development and underdeveloped infrastructure has become increasingly acute.

Figure 8.5: Garden City, Nanchang

Improvement of the Supervision System for Sustainable Development

Proposed real-time environment monitoring networks and an environment safety pre-alarm system have not yet been installed. Natural ecological protection and administration systems also need to be strengthened.

The rapid development of the economy brings new pressures to the ecological environment system. Some towns have set up Industrial Development Zones without comprehensive investigation, which results in the emergence of high energy-consuming and high pollution enterprises.

Strategy and Implementation in Constructing a Low-carbon City

The core of the strategic implementation plan is the Poyang Lake Ecological Economic Zone – constructing 'one base, three centres and four Nanchangs'.[1] The focus is a harmony between humans and nature, with quality of life as the starting point. In practical terms, there has to be an alignment between industrial structure, the resource utilisation rate and the environment of mountains, rivers, and lakes.

Figure 8.6: Photovoltaic Cells, Nanchang

Constructing a Low-carbon Industrial System

Nanchang puts industrial transition and upgrade as a strategic priority. The development of four low-carbon industries is at the forefront: solar photovoltaic, green illumination, service outsourcing, and cultural tourism.

The city seeks to develop six new low-carbon industries: new-energy cars, modern logistics, aviation manufacturing, new-energy equipment, biomedicine, and new materials.

It also strives to reduce the carbon dioxide emissions from four high-carbon industries: ferrous metal smelting and rolling/processing, chemical materials and chemical manufacturing, non-metallic mineral production, and paper production.

Nanchang also actively promotes low-carbon agriculture through the 'Million Mu of Fine Land' project to increase agricultural land output and comprehensive efficiency.

In the development of the service industry, Nanchang focuses on the modern finance service industry, modern tourism, logistics, trade and commerce, the trade service industry, and the information service industry.

Constructing a Low-carbon Energy System

Nanchang has strengthened the economy by improving the resource utilisation rate and reducing energy consumption and waste emissions. At the same time, the city is altering the structure of energy supply by halting the construction of thermal power plants, limiting the expansion of existing thermal power plants, and improving electricity-generating efficiency. Therefore, by changing both the power consumption and supply modes, Nanchang has tried to match low-carbon power with low-carbon industry.

Improving Low-carbon Space Layout

Urban transition means changing the urban space layout, including replanning the existing urban space structure, and designing new urban space. Nanchang pinpoints and utilises the natural carbon-bearing capacity. It connects wetlands, lakes, forest, and parks, and seeks to achieve an urban ecological carbon-bearing network.

The low-carbon city becomes visible through solar roofs, solar street lights, three-dimensional gardens, electrical bus stations, green buildings, and waste sorting.

Nanchang has a Transit-oriented Development (TOD) strategy to build a new transportation network that interconnects both urban and rural areas. With subway transportation as the centre, it strengthens the seamless connection between the slow-transportation system and the subway. Nanchang strictly executes the emission standards for motor vehicles and encourages the use of new-energy vehicles.

The planning and layout of Nanchang's urban space accepts the template of the city's geography to shape its environmental priorities.

Constructing Low-carbon Buildings

With the emphasis on saving energy, water, and land; materials; and reusing energy, Nanchang strictly implements such standards in new buildings. Nanchang also initiates the renovation of existing high-energy consumption buildings. To renovate existing buildings, Nanchang has set up a real-time monitoring system of energy consumption for government buildings and large public buildings. It implements an energy audit and quota management mechanisms for these buildings.

Constructing Carbon Fixing and Reducing Carriers

Based on its own natural features, Nanchang constructs a 'mountain–river–city–lake' basic ecological framework. Nanchang is actively constructing carbon fixing and reducing carriers besides carbon emissions. The city is trying to restore ecological resources in Water Resource Reservation Zones and forests. It develops protection for and low-carbon tourism in wetland and forest resources. The Nanchang Low-carbon Development Plan (2008–20) was implemented to set up developing goals and timetables (Table 8.1).

Figure 8.7: Yao Lake Wetland Park, Nanchang

Table 8.1: Goals of Ecological City Construction in Nanchang

SN	Item	Unit	Current Value (2006)	Short-term Goal (2010)	Mid-term Goal (2015)	Long-term Goal (2020)	Standard for Ecological Cities
1	Farmers' Average Yearly Income	CNY/person-year	4,392	5,700	≥11,000	≥15,000	≥8,000
2	Percentage of the Tertiary Industry in GDP	%	39.2	≥42	≥45	≥48	≥40
3	Energy Consumption Per Unit of GDP	Tons of standard coal/CNY10k	1.05*	≤1.0	≤0.9	≤0.8	≤0.9
4	Consumption of Fresh Water with Each 10k Increase of Yuan Industrial Production	m³/CNY10k	None	≤30	≤20	≤20	≤20
	Effective Usage Coefficient of Agricultural Irrigation Water		None	≥0.7	≥0.55	≥0.55	≥0.55
5	Percentage of Enterprises Required for the Permission of Compulsory Clean Production	%					
6	Forest Coverage	%	17.1	≥21.5	≥23.5	≥25	≥15
7	Percentage of Protected Area in Total Land Areas	%	–	≥10	≥15	≥17	≥17
8	Air Environment Quality	–	Meets the standard	Meets the standard	Meets the standard	Meets the standard	Meets the standard of the functional zone
9	Water Environment Quality	–	Meets the standard	Meets the standard	Meets the standard	Meets the standard	Meets the standard of the functional area and there is no inferior V-type water
10	SO₂ Emission Intensity Per CNY10 GDP	kg/CNY10k	3.14*	≤3	≤2.5	≤2.5	≤5.0
	COD Emission Intensity Per CNY10 GDP		5.87*	≤5	≤4.5	≤4	≤4.0
11	Water Qualification Rate of Central Drinking Water Source Area	%	99.8	100	100	100	100

SN	Item	Unit	Current Value (2006)	Short-term Goal (2010)	Mid-term Goal (2015)	Long-term Goal (2020)	Standard for Ecological Cities
12	Centralised Processing Rate of Urban Household Rubbish	%	69.44	≥80	≥85	≥90	≥85
	Reuse Percentage of Industrial Water	%	–	≥60	≥70	≥80	≥80
13	Noise Environment Quality	%	64.68	≥75	≥90	Meets the standard	Meets the standard
14	Harmless Treatment Rate of Urban Household Rubbish	%	100	100	100	100	≥90
	Treatment and Reuse Rate of Industrial Solid Waste	%	91.46	≥90	≥95	≥95	≥90
15	Average Urban Public Green Area Per Capita	km²/person	7.84	≥10	≥12	≥14	≥11
16	Percentage of Environment Protection Investment Against GDP	%	≥3.5*	≥3.5	≥3.5	≥3.5	≥3.5
17	Urbanisation Rate	%	53.7*	≥60	≥65	≥70	≥55
18	Public Satisfaction Ratio to Environment	%	80*	>90	≥92	≥95	≥90

Note: Data labelled * is sourced from *Nanchang Statistic Yearbook* (2005).[2]

Quoted from Nanchang Low-carbon Development Plan (2008–20).

Endnotes

1   One base: a modern manufacturing base. Three centres: logistics, commerce and trade, finance. Four Nanchangs: open and vigorous Nanchang, polite and harmonious Nanchang, reliable and pioneering Nanchang, ecological and garden Nanchang.

2   Nanchang Statistical Yearbook (2005), http://www.yearbookchina.com/ navibooklist-N2005100091-1.html

QINGDAO: TOWARDS A BLUE ECONOMIC ZONE

Qingdao has numerous natural, economic, and historical advantages in developing its own specific urban pathway in close relation to its maritime position. The city was a 19th-century treaty port, as the European powers recognised the quality of its harbour and its significant location on the East China Sea. The city still has distinctive European architecture alongside fine examples in the Chinese tradition.

Qingdao has a large and protected harbour, a beautiful coastline, and is ideally situated for seaborne exchange with the key economies of Japan and South Korea – both of which have a significant presence in the regional economy. Allied to its traditional trading role, the city has concentrated on research and development, putting the city at the forefront of new maritime industries.

An Overview of Qingdao

Qingdao is located in the south of the Shandong Peninsula, bordered to the east and south by the Yellow Sea, to the northeast by the city of Yantai, on the west by the city of Weifang, and to the southwest by the city of Rizhao. The total area of the city is 11,282 km². The sub-provincial city of Qingdao has direct jurisdiction over six districts and four county-level cities. Shinan (市南区), the old downtown, is located in the south of Qingdao city proper. The new downtown of Shibei (市北新区) lies in the centre of the city while

Licang (李沧区) is located further up the peninsula on the city's outskirts. At the end of 2014, the city's total population was 9,046,200, of which 4,875,900 made up the urban resident population. From 2012 to 2014, Qingdao was the twentieth, fourteenth, and eighteenth respectively in the ranking list of China's Urban Transformation and Upgrading Capability.

According to the Qingdao Master Plan (2011–20), the urban population of the central city will be 6.1 million by 2020, the urban construction land area will be 660 km², and the per capita construction land area will be 108 m².

Qingdao is an important tourist city with a rich cultural heritage. The old west part of the city is redolent of Qingdao's past as a German treaty port. The eastern district is in a modern international urban style. The middle part of the city has strong elements of the Jiaodong style of folk culture, and the outskirts of the city have many ancient cultural sites.

In 2014, the city's GDP was CNY869.21 billion, a per capita GDP of CNY96,524. The added value of primary industry accounted for CNY36.26 billion, the added value of secondary industry was CNY388.24 billion, and that of tertiary industry was CNY444.71 billion. The ratio of the three sectors was 4.2:44.6:51.2.

Figure 9.1: Qingdao Olympic Sailing Centre

Figure 9.2: Ba Da Guan Treaty Port Architecture in Qingdao

Qingdao has excellent bays and coastal resources. Its port was founded in 1892 and is now operated by a state-owned enterprise. Qingdao's historical success lies in its advantageous coastal position with a harbour which is wide, deep, and navigable all year round. Qingdao's status first as one of 14 approved coastal port cities from April 1984 and then as one of 15 sub-provincial cities from February 1994 has made it an important international trade port and sea transport hub.

This makes Qingdao one of the most important economic centres on the east coast of China. As the central city of the Shandong Peninsula city cluster, Qingdao has the following foci: a centre for company headquarters, an R&D centre, brand economy, exhibition economy, information service industry, commerce, trade flow, and all kinds of manufacturing service industry. All this provides a high-end platform for the economic development of Shandong.

From the perspective of traditional industry, Qingdao is competitive in locomotive vehicles, shipbuilding, marine industry, electronics and home appliances, petrochemical processing, car manufacturing, machinery, rubber, steel and iron, food, and light industry. In terms of new industry, Qingdao is developing marine industry, biological medicine, helicopter manufacturing, new energy, new materials, packaging innovation, and software.

Urban Space Restructuring and Expansion

The development and evolution of urban space should be a function of urban, economic, and social development. Qingdao's urban space structure has evolved in three main phases:

■ **A long period from 1891 to 1988, when its special expression had distinct belt features.** In the early part of this period when Qingdao was occupied by Germany (1898–1914), it developed along the east shore of Jiaozhou

Figure 9.3: Qingdao Harbour

Gulf from south to north. From 1949 to the end of 1980, Qingdao's urban structure followed the original belt-shaped spatial layout. The main urban area was highly developed, but not so the immediate rural hinterland, which seriously hindered the balanced development of the city.

From 1989 to 2002, when the city shifted from 'belt' shape to '∠' shape. From 1989, adjustment to the original urban general planning pushed development along Jiaozhou Gulf. The east and west wings of Jiaozhou Gulf developed quickly and the central urban district was transformed from a 'belt' shape to the shape of a Chinese character '品'. In 1995, the general planning office defined the urban general layout as 'two districts and one cluster'. The east shore of Jiaozhou Gulf was the main urban district, the west shore was the auxiliary district, and the district along Jiaozhou Gulf would form a cluster. In this way, the urban structure feature was 'relatively concentrated and appropriately dispersed'.

From 2002 to the present Qingdao has expanded from the shape of '∠' to the shape of 'Ω' as a result of important decisions made by the Qingdao Municipal Government. First, growth to the west made the shape of '品'. This was followed by expansion to the north, characterised as 'one gulf, two wings, and three poles', and the strategy was called 'development along the gulf'.

In November 2007, Qingdao Municipal Government put forward the strategy of 'development along Jiaozhou Gulf'. A bigger urban framework with 'one main district, three auxiliary districts, and multi clusters' came into being, along with urban development based in the main district – developing the city along the gulf with radiation

Figure 9.4: Jiaozhou Qingdao Bay Bridge

towards all clusters. The strategy of 'development along the gulf' is in essence an industrial spatial expansion strategy. After the east expansion in the 1990s and the west shift in the early 21st century, advancing towards the north and developing along the gulf is inevitable under the national rigid restraint of land resources. The core strategy is to help the city reclaim land from the sea.

Developing a Marine Economy and Building the Blue Economic Zone

Basic Conditions for the Construction of the Blue Economic Core Area

In the early 1990s, Shandong Province implemented the 'Sea Strategy of Shandong'. At the beginning of 2011, the State Council officially approved the Shandong Peninsula Blue Economic Zone Development Plan – the first regional development strategy focusing on marine economy in China. The approval for the implementation of the Plan means regional development extending from the land economy to the marine economy. The construction of Shandong Peninsula Blue Economic Zone is part of a national strategy, with Qingdao City leading.

Qingdao has four major advantages in the development of such a zone:

- **Its good geographical location and natural resources.** Across the East China Sea lie the large economies of Japan and South Korea, while to the west Qingdao can serve the extensive Yellow River Basin area. Qingdao's marine hinterland comprises offshore seas of 1.22 million km², tidal flats of 375.3 km², and coastline of 711 km. In the vicinity are 69 islands and 49 natural harbours. There are abundant marine biological resources. Qingdao is a perfect combination of 'mountain, sea, city, culture, and business'.

- **Not surprisingly, Qingdao has strong capacity in marine science and technology.** It has 28 marine scientific research and development institutions, accounting for one-third of those in China. There are more than 5,000 professional and technical personnel in Qingdao.

- **The geographical and natural environment also encourages marine industry.** Marine fishery, port logistics, ship manufacturing, and

Figure 9.5: Qingdao Liuting International Airport

coastal tourism are all on the increase. More recently, marine biological products, marine drugs, and seawater desalination have emerged and thrived. In particular, the output of marine biological pharmaceutical products accounts for 40 per cent of China's production.

- **Infrastructure is being developed to take advantage of these natural benefits and economic development.** In 2012, the cargo throughput reached 0.4069 billion tons. This and container throughput are now among the world's top ten. Take-off and landing capability at Qingdao Liuting International Airport has reached 4E class standards, and its airport passenger throughput in 2010 reached 10 million people. The construction of a second airport, Qingdao Jiaodong International Airport, began in 2015 as a 'regional hub airport, the gateway to Japan and South Korea'. The highway traffic mileage of Qingdao, over 17,000 km in 2015, ranks first place among the national sub-provincial cities.

The Progress in Building the Blue Economic Core Area

Qingdao has become an exemplar of the 'Blue Economy, high-end manufacturing and strategic new emerging industry'.[1] While the scale of marine economy is increasing in general, the structure of three particular sectors has been optimised and has become the driving force for the transformation and upgrading of Qingdao.

The scale of the marine economy is increasing rapidly year on year. The output value of the marine economy increased from CNY66.5 billion in 2009 to CNY175.11 billion in 2014, accounting for 20.2 per cent of GDP. The four pillar industries are coastal tourism, marine transportation, marine equipment manufacturing, and relevant material manufacturing, whose output value reached CNY116.63 billion yuan, accounting for 66.6 per cent of the marine economy.

The industrial structure of marine industry has been optimised through a shift towards the secondary and tertiary sectors. In 2014, the added value from the primary industry of marine economy was CNY9.41 billion, from secondary industry of marine economy was CNY79.81 billion; and from tertiary industry of marine economy was CNY85.89 billion. The ratio of the three sectors within the marine economy was then 5.4:45.6:49.1.

Towards the Blue Economy

The ultimate aim of Qingdao's new form of marine or 'blue' economy is to become a model city that can realise harmony between human beings and the sea. According to the Shandong Peninsula Blue Economic Zone Development Plan, by 2020 Qingdao will have become a regional centre of marine industry, Northeast Asia international shipping, and international marine science and technology education, as well as an international coastal tourist and maritime sports resort.

Measuring the Development of the Blue Economy

Seeing the whole picture to optimise layout. Within the urban spatial strategy, Qingdao has now completed the overall plan of its Blue Economy Development Zone with three specific elements: the West Coastal Economic Zone, Blue Silicon Valley, and the Red Island Economic Zone. This is supported by 17 special plans and 12 urban district plans. The West Coast Economic Area will be a 'high-end international marine industry gathering area, international shipping hub, marine economy demonstration area of international cooperation, national land and sea rural development pilot area, and Shandong Peninsula Blue Economic Zone pilot area'.[2] In order to make full use of the unique advantages of marine science and technology, the Blue Silicon Valley will be a world-class centre of research and development, talent agglomeration, and marine industry training. The Red Island Economic Zone will also be a key area for technology, and an ecological and cultural city.

Figure 9.6: West Coast Economic Zone

Figure 9.7: Ocean University of China, Located in Blue Silicon Valley

A transformative conceptual shift to make marine resources the centre of economic development. Pilot reforms in the fields of finance, ocean transportation, shipping, and administration are significant because marine industry demands high input, and has high risks and a long return cycle on investment. In 2012, in order to solve the financing issue Qingdao became a debt financing pilot city with the authorisation to pick several qualified SMEs to issue interbank bonds. And now Qingdao has become one of the second group of pilot cities entitled to facilitate cross-border CNY settlement. The long-term significance is that the West Coast Economic Zone is set to take the lead in adjusting administrative divisions in accordance with the principle of simplification, unification, and efficiency. At the same time, Qingdao Municipal Administration has transferred more than 300 items of administrative approval authority to lower levels.

Opening-up and cooperation is seen as the driving force to gather resources from all over the world. Qingdao tries its best to promote multilevel, all-round domestic, and international cooperation. The West Coast Economic Area is positioned in Qingdao's International Economic Cooperation Zone, within which there is a Sino–German Ecopark that promotes green building and low-carbon industry. Cooperation among the governments of the Blue Economic Zone of Shandong Peninsula can achieve mutual benefits for all the participants.

New innovative platforms to implement the 'Blue Silicon Valley' strategy. In 2011, Qingdao established the 'Blue Silicon Valley' strategy. Now it has been incorporated into the national marine economic development plan. The platform of marine industry includes the functions of R&D and incubation, attracting top marine scientific research institutions and enterprises. Many national innovation platforms have been set up including the National Deep-sea Base, Qingdao Ocean Science and Technology National Laboratory,

and Qingdao Marine Geology Research Institute. Relying on these innovation platforms, there already have been scientific and technological achievements. For example, the 'Kexue' Research Vessel – the most advanced comprehensive marine science survey ship in China – has been put into use. The deep-sea submersible named 'Dragon' has successfully dived to deeper than 7,000 m.

Complexes of 'scientific research, production and marketing', to promote the cooperation between government, research institutes, and industry. The Blue Economy needs intensive investment of technology, talents and capital. On the basis of science and technology platforms, Qingdao promotes the establishment of a series of 'scientific research–production–market' complexes to promote the industrialisation of scientific and technological achievements. For example, Qingdao Better Biological Technology Co., Ltd makes investments to incubate and proceed pilot plant tests on scientific and technological achievements. The company has implemented large-scale production in the industrial park, turning ordinary dried shrimp into biological products and then exports to Europe and the United States.

An industrial pathway with a clear direction: 'leading project – industry chain – industrial cluster – industrial park'. Qingdao continues to improve its industrial parks' carrying capacity. It promotes the concentration of marine industry projects, so the industrial parks become important carriers of 'enterprises, industrial clusters, relevant resources, and administrative functions'.

Figure 9.8: 'Kexue', the Comprehensive Marine Science Survey Ship

Figure 9.9: Model of 'Dragon' Deep-sea Submersible, www.quanjing.com

Endnotes

1   Blue Economic Zone Planning of Shandong
    Peninsula, http://news.shm.com.cn/2011-02/16/
    content_3385066.htm

2   Qingdao West Coast Economic Zone Development
    Plan, http://sdcom.gov.cn/public/html/news/352136.
    html (accessed 26 April 2018).

HANGZHOU: A PARADISE ON EARTH

10

Hangzhou is famous, along with Suzhou, as one of the most beautiful cities in China, not only for its natural setting – the West Lake – but also because of its gardens and historic buildings. Hangzhou is also the capital of Zhejiang, one of the most prosperous provinces in China, and along with Shanghai and Nanjing (capital of Jiangsu), is a key player in the Yangtze Delta Economic Zone.

The prosperity of Zhejiang, its proximity to Shanghai, its distinctive urban landscape centred on the West Lake, and its fast-rising university all make it very attractive to high-tech industry and entrepreneurs seeking economic opportunity and quality of life. In order to realise this potential, Hangzhou planners have had to rethink the pattern of urban expansion to allow development while still foregrounding the city's historic advantages.

Hangzhou has a long history. It became a well-known commercial and important trade port as early as the Tang Dynasty. It is one of the seven ancient capitals of China and has a documented history of more than 2,200 years. There is even evidence of human habitation in Hangzhou 4,700 years ago. The city has many beautiful scenic spots and historic sites, such as West Lake and Xixi Wetland Park.

In 1183, the Southern Song Dynasty decided to move the capital to Hangzhou, and it soon became a national political, economic, educational, and cultural centre. From then, along with Suzhou, the city was known as a 'Paradise on Earth'. Throughout succeeding dynasties the city was both an important trading hub and a cultural and tourism centre. These features defined its development: the 'integration of lake and city'.

Since 1949, especially during the past 30 years of economic reform and opening-up, the city has developed rapidly. However, this economic expansion has come increasingly into conflict with its original function and layout. Since 1980, development took place in a relatively small geographical area around the West Lake, the historical centre of Hangzhou's cultural and aesthetic legacy. Therefore, the key point of Hangzhou's transformation is to break the old development pattern, and to reconsider the relationship between the landscape and economic development.

The Background of Transformation Development

Hangzhou is located in the north of Zhejiang Province and near the southeast coast of China. The city sits on the north shore of the Qiantang River at the southern end of the Beijing–Hangzhou Grand Canal.

Figure 10.1: West Lake, Hangzhou

Hangzhou is one of the most important transport-hub cities in Southeast China and is sub-provincial. At the end of 2013, the total area of Hangzhou was 16,596 km², and the municipal district area was 3,068 km². The total population was 8.844 million, and the municipal district population was 6.3562 million. According to Hangzhou City Overall Planning (2001–20),[1] the city aims to be the pioneer area of Beautiful China. By 2020 the resident population in Hangzhou will be controlled within 10 million while that in the central urban area will be controlled within 4 million. By 2020 the urban and rural construction land will be controlled within 1119 km², among which the urban construction land will be controlled within 729 km² and that in the central area will be controlled within 430 km². In 2014, the city's GDP was CNY920.12 billion, and the per capita GDP was CNY103,757, placing it in the top ten in China. The primary sector accounted for an added value of CNY27.44 billion, the secondary sector added value was CNY385.89 billion, and the tertiary sector added value was CNY506.79 billion.

This gives the following economic structure – 3.0:41.9:55.1. From 2012 to 2014, Hangzhou took, respectively, the fifth, sixth, and seventh position in China's Urban Transformation and Upgrading Capability list.

The Evolution of City Function

After the founding of the PRC, Hangzhou made great strides as both a scenic tourist city, and as the political, economic, and cultural centre of Zhejiang Province. During the 'First Five-year' period, industrial production expanded rapidly. During the 'Second Five-year' period, the city function was transformed from a single consumer service-based city to a comprehensive production-based city, and this had a profound influence on the city's later development.

On 12 March 2001, the State Council officially approved the revocation of the county-level Xiaoshan City and Yuhang City and merged them into Hangzhou as Xiaoshan District and Yuhang

Table 10.1: Area and Population of Subdivisions

No.	Subdivision	Population (2013)	Area (km²)
City Proper			
1	Shangcheng District	351,300	18
2	Xiacheng District	531,400	31
3	Jianggan District	1,016,300	210
4	Gongshu District	561,000	88
5	Xihu District	833,500	263
6	Binjiang District	326,300	73
Suburban			
7	Xiaoshan District	1,535,200	1,163
8	Yuhang District	1,201,200	1,222
9	Fuyang District	725,500	1,808
County			
10	Tonglu County	410,200	1,780
11	Chun'an County	341,400	4,452
County-level Cities			
12	Jiande	436,900	2,364
13	Lin'an	573,800	3,124

Source: *Hangzhou Statistical Yearbook* (2014)[2]

District. In December 2014, the State Council approved the revocation of the county-level Fuyang City and merged it into Hangzhou as Fuyang District. These adjustments of city boundaries have provided new chances for the city. Hangzhou strengthened its functions of comprehensive service competitiveness, has intensively developed its technology industries, and turned greater attention to its environment.

The Expansion of City Space

The spatial expansion took place in two stages. The first was an expansion encircling the West Lake.

At the end of the 1950s, under the slogan 'developing the economy, securing supplies', industrial production expanded rapidly. Large industrial zones appeared on the outskirts of Hangzhou. As the centre grew, these industrial zones became connected with the centre. This spontaneous expansion has made the central city much bigger and the regional spatial structure has become more and more complicated.

In the early 1990s, the city entered a rapid development period, while the spatial expansion faced new problems as land was scarce. This trend was more serious after 1992. The sprawling expansion together with intensive construction on the outskirts brought new problems, such as the phenomenon of 'villages within the city', areas of rural status surrounded by an urban environment, as well as the loss of farmland in the suburbs. There were three consequences: the city centre became less attractive for tourism, high-end services did not develop at the same rate, and the city's aesthetic and cultural qualities became endangered.

The development of Hangzhou reflects the traditional growth path of big Chinese cities. The contradiction between city function and spatial layout is not simply the problem of 'using land'. In essence, it is that the process of urbanisation lags behind industrialisation, and city development lags behind economic development. Hangzhou's policymakers have reinterpreted the relationship between the city and economic development.

The Challenges of Transformation

City Planning

For a long time, Hangzhou developed around the West Lake and, taking the old city as the centre, spread outward in a circular expansion. With the increase of population this could not be sustained and led to urban decay. The task was to find new ways of using the available space with a new layout and overcome the limitations of operating from a single and historically defined city centre.

City Construction

Previously, big buildings, roads, and overpasses were the symbols of modernisation. City administrators adopted the method of 'reconstruction of the old city' to remove old buildings, streets and the old downtown to build a new city, in other words, tearing it down. The new city was akin to a cement jungle. This resulted in serious damage to the traditional city features, cuts off the city's historical context, and erases its individuality – one size fits all. The problem was how to grow the city space without losing its specificity as a place. Given its historic beauty and significance this is a core issue for Hangzhou.

City Management

The urban area has expanded from the original 683 to 3,068 km². It has become a city with a resident population of 8.7 million. Rapid urbanisation increases the difficulty of city management. How to update the idea of city management and optimise the city management system is a major challenge. On the other hand, the spatial expansion is an opportunity to reimagine the whole city and the relationship of the parts to each other and to the whole.

Industrial Structure Adjustment and Upgrading

Hangzhou is a city with few natural resources, and although once a port city its historic canal is unsuitable for a modern economy. Given its role as a historic and cultural centre, heavy industrial development is also unsuitable. At the same time, as the capital of one of China's richest provinces Hangzhou has seen its per capita GDP leaping from $10,000 to $20,000. Aligning this prosperity with an appropriate industrial upgrading is a key task for the city administrators.

City Traffic

From 1999 to 2014, the number of Hangzhou's motor vehicles has risen from 0.338 million to 2.54 million. Although Hangzhou has implemented a series of road improvement works in recent years, the city road construction is far behind the growth of motor vehicles, and traffic gridlock is a serious problem.

City Housing

There are still many families, vulnerable groups, and low-income earners who cannot buy commercial housing or even affordable housing and this is exacerbated by Hangzhou's prosperity and its attraction for better-off residents. The housing problems for two 'sandwich-class' groups are especially prominent:

- Those low-income families who can neither meet the requirements of low-rent housing nor afford to purchase affordable housing.

- Those low-income families who can neither meet the requirements to purchase affordable housing nor afford commercial housing.

In addition, there are a large number of 'new Hangzhou' – those who dwell in the 'villages within the city'.

'Villages in the City'[3]

The city's spatial expansion has enveloped a number of villages that retain their rural status. The holding of rural tenure enables the original villagers to sublet – often extremely ramshackle – housing to migrant workers. These then become areas of severe economic and social deprivation.

City Public Governance

In modern society, government is no longer the only body of public governance. Social organisations, enterprises, and individuals have become important players and partners. Developing new models of community participation and institutional cooperation is crucial to the transformation of government functions and innovation in social management.

City Ecological Environment

In 2011, China began to implement a revised version of the 'ambient air quality standard'. The new national standard includes a density of PM2.5 and the density of ozone concentration per eight hours. The urbanisation here is to protect the environment, and to balance a 'mountain of gold and silver' with a scene of 'green water and the mountain'.

Hangzhou's Transformation in Practice

Hangzhou's future economic, social, and environmental success is bound up with the ability to take its historic attributes and use them with a sophisticated high-end economy. There needs to be a symbiotic relationship between the heritage

Figure 10.2: Village in the City, Hangzhou

and the advanced economy to create a new cultural dynamic.

Promoting the City's Organic Renewal

In recent years, Hangzhou has not only absorbed the prescriptions of city renewal theory, it has also learned practical, and negative, lessons of 'destroying the old and building the new' from the experience of other cities. The biological concept of the 'organism' has found its way into city construction. Hangzhou insists on eight guiding principles for its development: people-orientation, protection first, ecological priority, cultural emphasis, integrated composition, quality first, intensification and resource-saving, and historical sensitivity.

In 2001, Hangzhou began to formulate a new overall plan, adjusting the city's spatial layout in order to provide platforms to transform the

development. The current version of Hangzhou City Overall Planning (2001–20) insists on the idea of 'protecting the old city, and building a new city'. This involves changing the city development pattern from a circle form to a group form: 'city expansion towards the east, tourism towards the west, and development along and across the Qiantang River'.

From the beginning of the 21st century, Hangzhou has implemented three rounds of urban construction, called the 'Ten Big Projects'. Hangzhou insists on the principle of 'protection first, protecting all that should be protected'. For example, it has promoted the organic renewal of streets and buildings to retain the original, historic city features. It has implemented comprehensive protection projects for West Lake, Xixi Wetland, landmark cultural facilities, and University City. It has implemented a series of projects on road networks and city infrastructure

Figure 10.3: Xixi Wetland

Chinese Urban Transformation: A Tale of Six Cities

and comprehensive protection projects on ancient canals and urban rivers.

Xixi Wetland

In August 2003, Hangzhou launched the Xixi Wetland comprehensive protection project. By adjusting the density of buildings, and reducing the environmental carrying capability, the plant species have increased from 221 to 553; the resident species of fish and water birds have reached 50; and the species of other birds have increased from 79 to 142. The water quality in most areas of the wetland still remains third-class in quality standard, but there is improvement, and in some areas, second-class water quality standard has been achieved. The traditional farming and fishery culture is protected together with the renovation of old houses and the restoration of the unique human landscape. Xixi Wetland has been named 'China's most beautiful place' by *China National Geography*. In July 2009, it was selected as an international important wetland by Wetlands International and in January 2012, Xixi Wetland was awarded national 5A tourist attraction status

Building the '3+1' Modern Industrial System

Hangzhou's goal is to build a modern industrial system linking with the world and representing the characteristics of the city. This is a '3+1' modern industrial system: '3' is modern agriculture, industry, and service industry; '1' is cultural and creative industry.

For the purposes of development, the cultural and creative industries are considered a separate entity, as is a knowledge-intensive and intelligence-oriented industry whose distinctive features are 'brain + computer + culture'. From the beginning of the 21st century, Hangzhou proposed to develop the cultural and creative industries and emphasised eight categories: information services,

animation and game development, design services, new media, art, education and training, culture and leisure tourism, and a cultural exhibition centre.

In 2011, the city's added value from the cultural and creative industry hit CNY84.3 billion, 12 per cent of Hangzhou's GDP. In 2012, Hangzhou won permission from the United Nations Educational, Scientific and Cultural Organization (UNESCO) to join the Creative Cities of Global Networks. Hangzhou is the fifth city (for 'Craft and Folk Art') joining Santa Fe (USA), Aswan (Egypt), Kanazawa (Japan), and Icheon (Korea).

Developing the Economy by Developing the Urban Environment

Creating Growth Poles by Merging with the Yangtze River Delta

Regional Planning of the Yangtze River Delta proposes that Hangzhou should strive to build a 'high-tech industrial base, important international tourism and leisure centre, national cultural and creative centre, e-business centre, and regional financial services centre'.[4] Hangzhou aims to connect with Nanjing, in Jiangsu Province, and along with Shanghai will be a key player in the collective integration of the Yangtze River Delta.

In 2010, the opening of the Shanghai–Hangzhou Intercity High-speed Railway made the 'one city effect' much more obvious. An important connected action is the construction of East New Town in Hangzhou's east gate. The core area of East New Town is 9.3 km² with comprehensive functions including a traffic hub, high-end businesses, leisure and tourism services, and residential areas. East Railway Station is located at its centre. It has an area of 300,000 m² and had a total investment of about CNY12 billion.

Promoting High-end Industries by Constructing New Towns

Hangzhou is working around the concept of a 'compact city', which focuses on ideas of 'competitive, large scale, superior service, a beautiful environment, high quality'.[5] A prime example of this is the speedy construction of new towns, as the important platforms for the innovative industrial system. One example is Qianjiang New Town. This is located in the southeast of the downtown region, about 4.5 km away from the West Lake scenic region, and its planned area is about 21 km².

The transition from the 'West Lake era' to the 'Qiantang River era' was achieved between 2001 and 2008. The goal was to build 'a central business district, a new landmark for Hangzhou and a platform of modern service' through 'high-level planning, high-standard construction, high-intensity investment, and high-performing management'. This includes:

- a major public square;

- an underground cultural complex;

- a landscape platform;

- one bund (a scenic route along the river);

- 'two rivers' – the Xintang River and Jianggan River;

- 'two libraries' – Hangzhou New Library and Exhibition Hall of Hangzhou City Planning;

- 'two tunnels' – a new city tunnel and Qianjiang Tunnel;

- 'two theatres' – Hangzhou Grand Theatre and Hangzhou Branch of Chinese Chess;

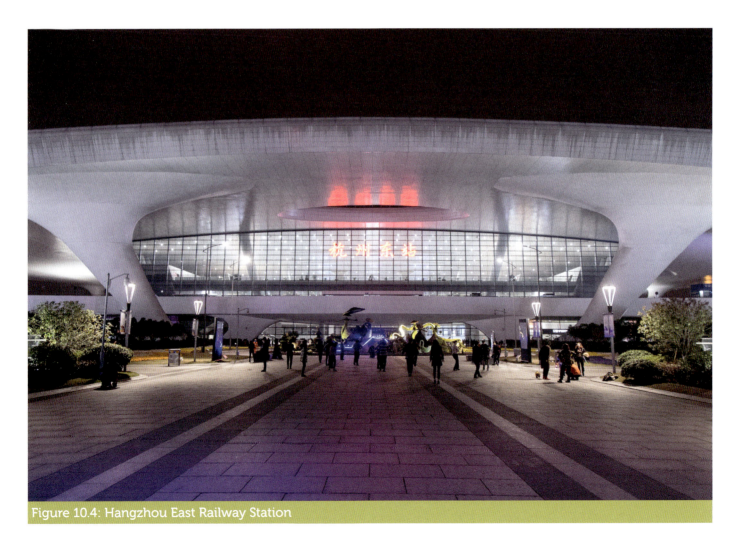

Figure 10.4: Hangzhou East Railway Station

- 'two parks' – Century Park and Forest Park;

- 'four centres' – a Public Centre, an International Conference Centre, Hangzhou Youth Development Centre, and Jianggan Culture and Sports Centre.

Developing the Economy by Constructing a City Complex and Commercial Buildings

The type and balance of buildings is a strategic choice that not only determines the city's spatial order but also its development path. The choice is between business buildings, commercial buildings, city complexes, scientific research buildings (including technological incubators), standard buildings for rent or sale, protected buildings (including historical architecture, old houses, industrial heritage, campus heritage), and rural dwelling SOHO.[6]

Hangzhou insists on moving towards a headquarters economy, alongside a cultural and creative one, plus a tax-sourcing one. For example, since 2011, the number of buildings whose tax revenue is over CNY100 million in Xiacheng District is more than 16.

Developing the Suburban Economy Through New Metropolitan Areas

A tough problem in Hangzhou is that in the past development has been unbalanced. The development of the eastern city is quicker and stronger than in the west; and there is further imbalance between urban and rural areas. The aim is to ensure that urban areas lead the development of rural areas, and eastern development drives forward the west. Since 2000, Hangzhou has accelerated the construction of metropolitan areas to promote balanced development.

Figure 10.5: Qianjiang New Town

Developing Headquarters by Improving the Business Environment

Since 2000, Hangzhou has firmly established the policy of 'environmental priority' and the philosophy that environmental investment gives the highest return. It strives to make Hangzhou the most attractive place to live in terms of culture, administration, and environment in order to attract first-class talent and enterprises. In 2013, 53 enterprises from Hangzhou were enrolled in the list of the Top 500 Chinese Private Enterprises, accounting for 38.1 per cent of those in the province, and 10.6 per cent in the country.

Making Hangzhou a Service-oriented City

With the process of urbanisation, the suburban industrial districts gradually become the central area of the city, and this brings problems. The intermixed layout of industrial enterprises and residential areas seriously limits quality of life. Some industrial enterprises occupy this golden land, but do not bring golden benefits.

At the beginning of 2002, Hangzhou implemented a 'relocation project for industrial enterprises'. By the end of 2010, the relocation of industrial enterprises from the old city had been largely completed. Hangzhou's landscape has been preserved, and the environment has been significantly improved. As a result, Hangzhou is now supremely attractive for residents, tourists, and key businesses.

Figure 10.6: Alibaba Group

Endnotes

1   Hangzhou City Overall Planning (2001–20),
    http://www.hzghy.com.cn/index.php/project/
    info/45/51

2   Hangzhou Statistical Yearbook (2014),
    http://tjj.hangzhou.gov.cn/content-
    getOuterNewsDetail.action?newsMainSearch.
    id=78139661-6229-11e8-97a6-d89d676397bf

3   Villages in the city: in the narrow sense, these are
    rural villages in the process of urbanisation. For the
    reason of land requisition, the peasants shift to be
    urban residents while the original villages evolve to
    be residential areas. In a broad sense, these are
    undeveloped residential areas in cities.

4   National Development and Reform Commission,
    Regional Planning of the Yangtze River Delta,
    http://www.ndrc.gov.cn/zcfb/zcfbghwb/201606/
    t20160603_806390.html (accessed 26 April 2018).

5   Wang Guoping. Promoting urban organic renewal
    and taking the road of scientific urbanization [J].
    Policy Outlook, 2008 (06):5–11

6   Rural dwelling SOHO: the place that rural and urban
    residents can live and work together, which is the
    symbol of the 'post industrialisation era' with
    Hangzhou characteristics. The rural dwelling SOHO
    creative park has attracted more than 100 cultural
    and creative enterprises including service design,
    film and television production, works of art, etc.

CHENGDU: TOWARDS A WORLD ECOLOGICAL GARDEN CITY

Chengdu is the historical and contemporary capital of Sichuan and has for centuries been the most significant city in Western China. This is of particular importance for China's domestic priority to develop the west and reduce its disparity with the eastern seaboard. More recently, the city has played an essential role in China's international agenda, epitomised by the One Belt and One Road Initiative.

Both domestic integration and the economic and political orientation towards Central Asia renew and enhance Chengdu's position as a major communication, logistics, and engineering centre. Allied to this is an initiative to establish Chengdu as a model of sustainable urban development. This draws on Chengdu's historical reputation for its quality of life and relaxed atmosphere, in accordance with a Chinese reading of Ebenezer Howard's *Garden Cities of To-morrow* (see page 119).

An Overview of Chengdu

Chengdu is the provincial capital and major city of Sichuan Province in Southwest China. It has huge significance for Western China and holds sub-provincial administrative status. Sichuan is located in the Silk Road Economic Belt and the Yangtze River Economic Belt. It plays a vital strategic role in bridging all geographic areas of China, and holds a crucial position in the construction of 'One Belt and One Road', a huge

economic expansion largely following the historic Silk Road through Central Asia into Europe. The city has an area of 12,390,000 km^2, is at its widest 192 km from east to west, and 166 km from north to south. It has a resident population of 14.0476 million, or 17.5 per cent of the total population of Sichuan.[1] In 2014, Chengdu was the first western city whose GDP surpassed CNY1 trillion. From 2012 to 2014, Chengdu took, respectively, the eleventh, thirteenth, and twelfth position in the ranking list of China's Urban Transformation and Upgrading Capability. According to Chengdu Overall Planning (2016–35), by 2035 the resident population in Chengdu will be about 23 million while that in the central urban area will be controlled within 13.6 million. By 2035 the urban and rural construction land will be controlled within 2,800 km^2, among which the urban construction land of Chengdu will be controlled within 2,070 km^2 and that in the central area will be controlled within 1,334 km^2.[2]

Between 1978 and 1990 Chengdu's urbanised rate moved slowly from 22.3 per cent to 27.3 per cent, increasing by 0.42 per cent each year. In 1985, the total GDP of the tertiary sector exceeded that of the primary sector for the first time, giving an economic structure of 'secondary, tertiary primary'. By 1990, the percentages of the contribution from the three sectors to the local GDP of Chengdu were respectively 20.9 per cent, 39.7 per cent, and 39.4 per cent. Since 1990, urbanisation has

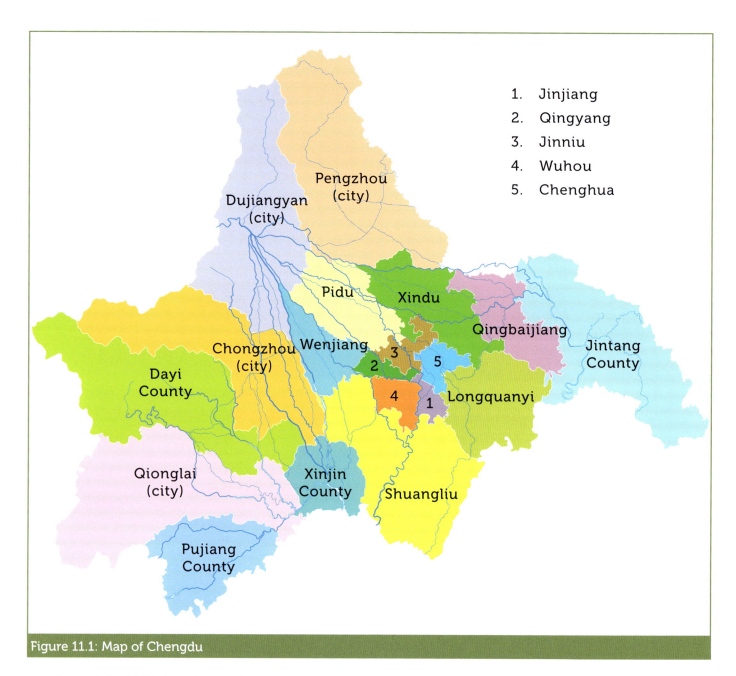

Figure 11.1: Map of Chengdu

Legend:
1. Jinjiang
2. Qingyang
3. Jinniu
4. Wuhou
5. Chenghua

accelerated. In 2006, its urbanisation rate reached 51.8 per cent, increasing year on year by 1.53 per cent. Chengdu now has a developed urban economy with the typical structure of 'tertiary, secondary, primary'. In 2013, the non-agriculture production of Chengdu accounted for 96.1 per cent of total GDP. Table 11.1 shows the structure percentage of Chengdu's three industries.

Chengdu has integrated the One Belt and One Road Initiative into its industrial layout plan. There are three strategic foci: the construction of a financial centre, the construction of a rail hub, and the development of an electronic information industry.

Figure 11.2: New Tianfu Square

Table 11.1: The Structure Percentage of Chengdu's Three Industries

Year	Structure Percentage of the Three Industries
1978	31.8:47.3:20.9
1980	27.2:49.7:23.1
1985	24.2:48.6:27.2
1990	20.9:39.7:39.4
1995	14.5:38.0:47.5
2000	10.1:36.5:53.4
2006	7.1 :44.0:48.9
2010	5.1 :44.7:50.2
2013	3.9 :45.9:50.2

Source: *Chengdu Statistical Yearbook* (2014)[3]

Chengdu is set to become the key regional financial centre on the upper reaches of the Yangtze River. In addition, Southwest Jiaotong University, located in Chengdu, is the top research centre for high-speed rail capability, and the city has successfully attracted investment from China Locomotive to upgrade its rail transportation manufacturing industry.

The electronic information sector has become the leading industry in Chengdu, with much of the sector moving from the coastal areas to the city, and also to Chongqing. By the end of 2014, in Chengdu 20 per cent of the world's computers were made, 50 per cent of the world's laptop computer chips had their package testing, and more than half of the world's iPads were manufactured.

Figure 11.3: Southwest Jiaotong University

Figure 11.4: Chengdu Hi-tech Zone

Building Chengdu's World Ecological Garden City

The Background and Objective of Building a World Ecological Garden City

The model for Chengdu's initiative is the Garden City movement initiated in the late 19th century by the British urban thinker Ebenezer Howard in *To-Morrow: A Peaceful Path to Real Reform* (revised in 1902 as *Garden Cities of To-morrow*).[4] This book described a kind of place that could enjoy the benefits of both a city – as opportunity, amusement, and good wages; and countryside – beauty, fresh air, and low rent.

Chengdu began to organise around the principles of an ecological city in 2007. In 2009, this was defined as the long-term objective of building a world ecological garden city within 20 years, and being recognised as a world city within 30–50 years. The core features of such a city are natural beauty, social justice, and urban–rural integration. It has four basic elements:

- A progression from national central city to regional central city in the world economy, and being finally recognised as a world city in its own right.

- Modernisation. Chengdu intends to make West China part of a globalised economic environment.

- Chengdu is set to become a multi-centre, clustered and networked city with a rural–urban spatial layout and a population of 20 million.

- Chengdu as a garden city will realise a harmony between city and countryside; a balance between modernity and heritage.

Fortune (Chinese version, 2014) released a list of China's most liveable cities for the retired. Chengdu ranked among the top three for five consecutive years. *Fortune* said: 'The rapid economic development is driven by the prosperity of the business and the growth of urban infrastructure. The liveable characteristics of Chengdu have been strengthened.'[5]

The Process of Building a World Ecological Garden City

The key components of this process are:

- Taking the central city as the core, Chengdu forms an urban–rural layout. Cities, towns, and villages are separated from each other by farmland.

- A corridor-like, clustered, and network-shaped rural–urban space layout forms 'green hills and blue waters surrounding bamboo groves, big cities and small towns embedded in farmland'.

Chengdu forms a modern industrial system with service industry and headquarters economy at the core, alongside high-tech technology industry, powerful modern manufacturing, and modern agriculture, thus:

- Modern agriculture is co-developed with secondary and tertiary industries, including tourism, logistics, commerce, and trade.

- The central city will house company headquarters and high-tech industry as well as high-end manufacturing industry.

- The central city will also site other aspects of the tertiary sector including financial services and a cultural and creative sector. Alongside the high-end manufacturing in the second and third layers will also be modern service industry, creative hubs, international trade and commerce, tourism, and logistics ventures.

There has to be a much more intensive use of resources with respect to both urban construction and industrial development.

- Intensive utilisation of resources. Into the 2020s, there will be a limit to land available for new construction. Consequently, there has to be intensive land utilisation. Moreover, Chengdu lacks water. Water has to be recycled and the limited sources used more effectively. Chengdu's power supply depends on external input so it also needs to be used more effectively.

- Intensive urban construction. Cities and towns are constructed in an intensive way. Central urban districts, with modern service industry as their main function, are in intensive spatial forms. Surrounding districts and new satellite cities aggregate around cluster centres and transportation hubs.

- Intensive industrial development. This is achieved by concentration on industrial parks with an industrial centralisation rate above 80 per cent. Intensive use of industrial land means increasing the floor area ratio of industrial land to above 1.5.

- Intensive rural area development. Chengdu aims to develop modern agriculture in a scaled and refined way, which focuses on high added-value agriculture with the use of compact buildings in rural areas.

Urban districts should have multiple functions for working, living, leisure, and transportation. This generates both economic vitality and liveability and fully utilises space both above and underground. A mixed environment also helps to create living communities which are rarely empty in the day, such as parks and residential areas; or at night, such as vacated business centres.

- People-centred spatial arrangement. By avoiding excessively wide streets and oversized squares, buildings in Chengdu have been allocated with appropriate street and lane space and open public space, as well as a variety of shops.

- People-centred function: medical care, education, cultural activities, shopping and entertainment, and other public services are provided in each area.

- People-centred infrastructure. Chengdu develops easy-to-use public infrastructure for the needs of the population.

There is a concern that the city's environment should include a relationship to the rural and the natural, summed up as 'mountain, water and farmland'.

- To this end, the nearby Longmen and Longquan Mountains are protected, so inhabitants have the feeling of 'living in the forest'.

- Farmlands in urban areas – farmlands are not only for agricultural production, but also have an ecological and leisure function.

- Parks and gardens – green land is spread throughout the city, including the centre, and the preservation of green spaces gives built-up areas the sense of being town rather than suburbs.

- The roads between cities and towns, and towns and villages follow the natural topography in order to give the landscape harmony.

- The distinctive Linpan culture in Western Sichuan, with its unique farm scenery and distinctive environmental characteristics, will be preserved.

- This also applies to the inherited and diverse spatial outline and different styles of architecture, dispelling homogeneity and anonymity.

Figure 11.5: Countryside in Chengdu

Figure 11.6: Chengdu Shuangliu Airport

Transport-oriented development comprises both linking the parts of Chengdu and linking Chengdu to national and international networks. Shuangliu International is Chengdu's second airport. It is an international airline hub with a passenger volume of 99 million each year. It also makes Chengdu – after Beijing and Shanghai – the third Chinese city to have two airports.

On the high-speed rail network Chengdu is the centre of a number of transportation circles. The two-hour circle takes in adjacent provincial capitals such as Guiyang and Kunming. A four-hour circle reaches out as far as Xi'an, Wuhan, and Lanzhou while an eight-hour transportation circle connects with the Bohai Economic Circle, Beijing–Tianjin–Hebei Economic Zone, the Yangtze River Delta, and the Pearl River Delta. Chengdu will also have direct rail links to West Asia, Europe, South Asia, and Southeast Asia.

- By road, 20 hours will encompass the Beijing–Tianjin–Hebei Economic Zone, the Yangtze River Delta, and the Pearl River Delta. Again, it will be a highway transportation hub that connects Central Asia, South Asia, West Asia, and Europe.

- The urban transportation network will integrate road, subway, and bus networks as well as the logistics infrastructure. The road network will be multilayered, with both ring and radial connections. The central city will be connected to counties by highways and expressways, counties connected to towns by national highways, and towns connected to villages by village-level roads.

- Both the subway and bus system integrate urban and rural elements of the overall city.

This develops a public service system and basic infrastructure that can cover both rural and urban areas. Chengdu emphasises the importance of meeting standards right across the city, in the following ways:

- Standardisation of supporting projects. It has different standards for supporting the construction of central cities, counties, key towns, ordinary towns, and new communities in rural areas. For example, there are nine categories each of about 100 items for supporting projects for central cities and counties. They include criteria for education, medical care, sports, culture, business, and government buildings.

- Standardisation of supporting functions. The standards of functioning facilities are established for a comprehensive range of social and public facilities including schools, medical care institutes, cultural facilities, sports facilities, and community service facilities. For example, the standards require that the relevant government departments should build high schools in cities, middle schools in towns, primary schools near villages, and central kindergartens in all towns. In the medical care system, for counties: comprehensive hospitals (plus specialist and Chinese medicine hospitals), community medical care centres, and community medical care stations. Comprehensive hospitals (plus specialist and Chinese medicine hospitals) or standard medical care centres for centre towns, standard medical care centres for other towns, and medical care stations for rural communities.

The Achievements and Features of Building a World Ecological Garden City

There have already been notable achievements. In urban construction, Chengdu has formed a spatial layout with core central urban areas, linking satellite cities, and supporting suburban central towns. In economic development, Chengdu has been continuously fast. Chengdu's GDP in 2014 had reached CNY1,005.66 billion, and the local finance budget revenue had reached CNY102.52 billion. The structure of the three industrial sectors has been optimised, and its industrial capability has

Figure 11.7: GDP and Growth Rate of Chengdu (2010–14)

Source: 2014 Statistical Bulletin of Chengdu National Economic and Social Development

been improved. It has made great progress in changing its development mode, especially in the fields of pollution reduction and energy saving.

Adhering to Overall Planning and Top-level Design

The coordination of planning and execution has been an important element of success.

Implementing overall planning and design helps to ensure coverage of all geographical areas, and the supervision of implementation. Chengdu emphasises consistency in economic and social development planning, industrial development, the general planning of towns, land utilisation planning, transportation development planning, and new village development planning. For example, Chengdu combines the construction of industrial parks with new towns to form an organic ecology.

Establishing the Administration Structure and Improving System Coordination

Chengdu has set up a committee for overall urban and rural development led by municipal leaders and involving the participation of related departments. Based on the concept of city and industrial integration, Chengdu selects some cities and towns that have a solid industrial basis as pilots for future development. For example, Chengdu Economic Development Zone, based on the existing car industry, synchronises the construction of infrastructure for the economic zone and for the town. In another case, Pujiang Shouan New Town seeks to implement a development mode that can integrate city and industry with ecological beauty. It actively pushes the integration of living areas and production areas, production areas and public leisure areas, and production areas and related service areas.

The Features of Building a World Ecological Garden City

These are as follows:

■ Industries and cities complement each other. The level of industry globalisation reflects the level of urban globalisation. Industry is concentrated in order to make the city both more productive and environmentally diverse.

■ Chengdu promotes urbanisation through opening-up and internationalisation. It aims to develop an international financial centre alongside its technology, trade and commerce, and logistics centre, resulting in a broader base for development.

■ Chengdu makes the ecological and aesthetic foundation of the city a priority. It emphasises the protection of mountains, rivers, land, and forests. It strives to develop and maintain organic connections between forests, parks, rivers, wetlands, and streets.

Shouan New Town

Pujiang County is a gateway in the southwest of Chengdu City. The county has an area of 583 km², and administers eight towns, four townships, and 132 villages. There is a total population of 2.63 million. The forest coverage reaches 49.5 per cent and the air quality is the best in Chengdu. Pujiang enjoys the reputation of 'Garden of Chengdu – Green Pujiang'. Based on its resource endowments and industrial foundations, Pujiang aimed to construct the 'most beautiful garden city' with features of 'good ecology, good urban–rural spatial form, good industrial system, and [a] high degree of satisfaction of the masses'.

It implemented the 'three bases with one axis' strategy to realise this target. 'Three bases' are 'the industrial base of modern agriculture, the manufacturing base of modern food and light industry, and a leisure tourism base for Chengdu'; the 'one axis' means 'a liveable city'. Shouan New Town, a town in Pujiang County, is a good example of the 'integration of urbanisation and industrialisation, and the integration of production and the city'. Shouan New Town has an area of 87.63 km², and 28 community and administrative villages. The population is 5.6 million people. Shouan's role in the development strategy is to be a national packing and printing industry base, and a sub-centre of the county's economic and social development.

■ In April 2010, Qing Pu Construction and Development Co., Ltd was founded as the operator of Shouan's industrialisation and urbanisation. The local government made the strategic decisions, and then established a market mechanism for long-term development. The bulk of investment and construction was transferred from government to market participants with the latter responsible for attracting investment.

■ The overall plan considers the optimisation of industrial parks and urban functions. Shouan New Town is regarded as an organic entity with overall consideration of economic, social, and ecological functions. There is an open-style industrial park with high-end complexes that seek to combine the multiple functions of business, research, and living. All in all it is an attempt to redefine the balance between life and work; the stability of society and the development of the economy.

■ Living space is found within the green industrial base. The aim is to balance three aspects: improving the industrial park and shaping the urban image, exploiting the industrial park, and constructing a new-type community.

Figure 11.8: Shouan New Town

Figure 11.9: Commercial Street with Chengdu Characteristics, Broad and Narrow Alley

As one of the leading Chinese historical and cultural cities, Chengdu seeks to manifest its Ba-shu culture in its urban renovation. It not only protects tangible historical streets and blocks, but also protects intangible cultural brands and urban cultural landmarks.

People-orientation is the starting point. The main purpose of urban development is to make better lives for more people. Close attention is paid to enhancing the daily lives of citizens through environmental improvement, public service, and social administration. Such a city will attract more talent to Chengdu and further enhance the quality of life for all.

Endnotes

1 The resident population refers to the actual population of a certain period of time (more than half a year, including half a year).

2 Chengdu Master Plan (2016–35), [EB/OL], http://www.cdgh.gov.cn/ (accessed 28 April 2018).

3 Statistical Bureau of Chengdu, *Chengdu Statistical Yearbook* (2014), http://www.cdstats.chengdu.gov.cn/htm/detail_52422.html (accessed 26 April 2018).

4 Ebenezer Howard, *To-Morrow: A Peaceful Path to Real Reform*, London: Swan Sonnenschein, 1898; Ebenezer Howard, *Garden Cities of To-Morrow*, Cambridge, MA: The MIT Press, 1965.

5 'China's most liveable cities for the retired', *Fortune* (Chinese version), 16 September 2014, http://www.fortunechina.com/rankings/c/2014-09/16/content_219769.htm (accessed 26 April 2018).

HEFEI: TOWARDS AN INNOVATIVE CITY

Hefei, like Nanchang, is not an especially well-known city but is more representative of the experience of the majority of China's urban dwellers. In 2016 China had an urban population of over 800 million while its five largest cities (Shanghai, Beijing, Chongqing, Tianjin, and Guangzhou) accounted for only 77 million, or less than 10 per cent of the urban population.

Most Chinese cities, like Hefei, must make their way according to national directives and with lobbying from the city upwards find their own niche following the prevailing priorities. Hefei is a city earmarked for 'innovation', with a transition from economic development based on primary and low-end secondary manufacturing to high value-added, research-based, and more sophisticated services. This is an aspiration shared not only by other Chinese cities but also by cities across the world. Hefei is then a case study in the possibilities and problems of implementing this strategy in a characteristic mid-sized city.

An Overview of Hefei

Hefei is the capital of Anhui Province. It is located in the middle of the province, adjacent to the Yangtze River Delta Economic Circle. It is a crucial city in the industrial shift between the coastal areas and the first tier of inland provinces. If Hefei is at the centre of a circle with a 500 km radius, the area embraces seven provinces or directly controlled municipalities. Since the administrational adjustment in August 2011, Hefei itself governs one county-level city, four counties, and four districts. It has three national-level Development Zones and 14 provincial Development Zones. Hefei has an area of 11,434.25 km^2 and a regular population of 7,611,000 according to the 2013 census. The constructed area is 339 km^2 and the regular urban population is 3.55 million. According to Hefei Overall Planning (2011–20), by 2020 in the central urban area, the resident population will be controlled within 3.6 million and the urban construction land within 360 km^2.[1]

合肥市城市总体规划（2011–2020年）

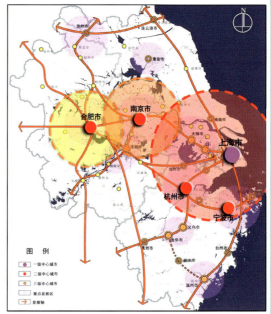

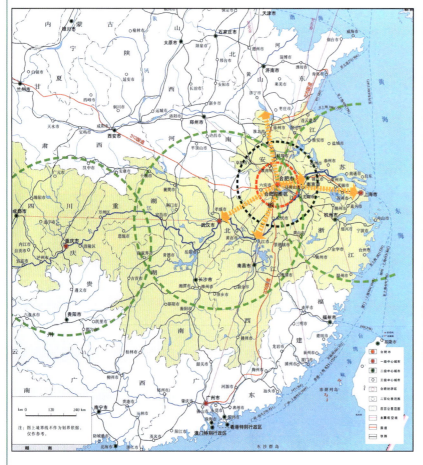

在全国的位置	在"长三角"的位置
交通区位	在"中四角"的位置

Figure 12.1: Location Map (Hefei)

Table 12.1 shows the GDP and percentage of the three industries from 1978 to 2013.[2] From 2012 to 2014, Hefei took, respectively, the twenty-eighth, thirty-seventh, and sixty-second position in the ranking list of China's Urban Transformation and Upgrading Capability. In 2013, Hefei's per capita GDP was CNY65,722.

Hefei is still primarily a manufacturing city. The aim is to enhance technological innovation in the industrial structure of the 'secondary: tertiary: primary' model.

Table 12.1: Hefei GDP and Its Structure (1978–2013)

Indicator	1978	1980	1985	1990	1995	2000	2005	2010	2012	2013
GDP (CNY100 million)	12.58	14.15	31.39	58.19	173.53	369.16	925.61	2701.61	4164.32	4672.91
Industrial Structure of Hefei	100.0	100.0	100.0	100.0	100.0	100.0	100.0	100.0	100.0	100.0
Primary Industry (%)	28.6	29.5	30.5	28.7	18.2	10.1	5.7	4.9	5.5	5.3
Secondary Industry (%)	49.6	48.0	47.6	45.3	46.1	44.0	45.9	53.9	55.3	55.3
Tertiary Industry (%)	21.9	22.4	21.6	26.0	35.7	45.9	48.4	41.2	39.2	39.4

Figure 12.2: Swan Lake CBD in Hefei

Building an Innovative City

The Background of Building an Innovative City

Hefei is one of the most important Chinese science and education bases. There are 60 academicians of the Chinese Academy of Science or China Engineering Academy in Hefei, 358 R&D institutions, 199 provincial key labs, 60 universities and colleges including the China Science and Technology University, 113 vocational schools, and 6.5 million university, college, and vocational school students. Although it has distinguished science and technology resources, Hefei's economic development has lagged behind for a long time. Its main industry was traditional manufacturing at the beginning of the 21st century, and the new industries didn't match its science and technology resources. Hefei had strong and advanced basic scientific research capability; however, its application capability has been comparatively weak. The task is how to make full use of its advantages.

In 1998, Jiang Zemin, secretary general of the CPC, visited the Hefei branch of the Chinese Academy of Sciences (CAS). He gave high marks to the scientific research and inscribed 'Science Island' for the Academy, which became its nickname. The following year, after visiting the science city of New Siberia in Russia, Jiang Zemin suggested to Lu Yongxiang, the president of the CAS, to transform the Science Island of Hefei into the Science City of China. In the first meeting of the Tenth National People's Congress in 2003, 16 representatives of Anhui Province proposed to transform Hefei into a science city. In November 2004, the Ministry of Science and Technology approved the selection of Hefei as a national pilot city of science and technology innovation following a decision by the State Council.

The aim was to use existing capability as a springboard to highlighting innovation platforms, enterprises, and a connected innovative industrial chain. Hefei now has a comprehensive industry system, from the traditional to the cutting edge:

Figure 12.3: Science Island, Hefei Branch of Chinese Academy of Sciences

including automobile assembly and manufacturing, home facility manufacturing, chemical and rubber tyre manufacturing, new materials, electronics information and software, biological technology and new medicine, and food and agriculture product processing. Its strategic emerging industries have expanded rapidly. In 2014, the output of strategic emerging industries reached CNY25.5 billion. This represents a 60 per cent contribution to the rate of industrial development.

The Process of Building an Innovative City

Hefei has set itself a number of targets: to transform the development mode via science and technology innovation, to increase the economic competitiveness via science and technology innovation, to grow into a national science and technology innovation city, and to become a science city with an international reputation by 2020.

Administrative Reform and Building a Service-Oriented Government

The pilot city project has a leading group from within the municipal committee and government. The city also established an operational office – the Hefei National Science and Technology Innovation Pilot City (Innovation Office). The Innovation Office issues an annual *Work Plan of the National Science and Technology Innovation Pilot City* and allocates tasks to relevant departments. The Innovation Office is responsible for evaluating their performance on an annual basis.

Hefei's leaders realised that science and technology innovation is a systematic process and that the pilot work cannot achieve significant progress without the appropriate administrative mechanisms.

Figure 12.4: Hefei Administration Service Centre

In 2006, the relevant officers of the main departments reported their administrative approval items and the legal basis for these items to all the top leaders in Hefei. Each item was evaluated in terms of whether it was legal, reasonable, necessary, or simple, and whether the process was convenient for the public. Only 230 items out of 353 were recognised as necessary. The Science and Technology Bureau became the first department that had no administrative approval items. Then 91 municipal departments made public their commitments about service items, working style, and efficiency.

By 2012, Hefei ranked fourteenth among Chinese cities for its comprehensive business environment according to *Fortune* (Chinese version).[3] Its business costs were the lowest among the top 50 emerging business cities. This is the result of the local government's efforts on cost control. In recent years, Hefei Municipal Government has vigorously delegated power to lower levels and deepened the reform of the administrative approval system. Therefore, it can increase administrative efficiency and improve government service capability.

Making Related Policies and Fostering an Innovative Environment

Hefei Municipal Government not only builds platforms for innovation investment, but also creates opportunities for the alliance between investors and innovators. This has four policy aspects: innovation, new industrialisation, modern services, and modern agriculture.

The policy system aims to upgrade the industrial structure and to develop the strategic emerging industries. For example, the innovation policy system focuses its attention on developing Hefei's science and technology industry, on effectively providing industrialisation services for Hefei's colleges, universities, and research institutions, on fostering new industrial clusters, on constructing innovation carriers, and on creating innovation talent hubs.

In July 2014, the strategy was organised around the '1+3+5' industry support system comprising one overall provision, three methods, and five major policies. The policy system consists of four types of funding support: investment funds, special subsidies, public financial products, and awards for successful fulfilment. For example, Anhui High-tech Power Technology Co., Ltd focuses on the research and development of 'power battery systems'. According to the '1+3+5' policy, it got financial support from the local government, which not only reduced the company's financial pressure, but also speeded up the progress of R&D.

Accumulating Financial Resources and Constructing an Innovation Industrial Chain

Hefei continually increases its public input into science and technology innovation. It actively encourages the initial public offering (IPO) of high-tech enterprises. The Hefei Science & Technology Rural Commercial Bank provides financing services for science and technology SMEs, amounting to CNY2 billion in loans annually. Anhui Industrial and Commercial Bank tries to carry out mortgage loans based on intangible assets and potential. In 2015, Hefei set up an insurance fund, which aimed to encourage insurance provision for scientific and technological innovation, and to share the innovation risk across all the participants.

Cultivating Innovation Enterprises and Strengthening Innovation Main Bodies.

After releasing *Science and Technology Innovation Enterprise Cultivation Plans* and *100 Enterprises Cultivation Project*,[4] Hefei selected a group of seed enterprises in selected fields, including new energy vehicles, public security, electronic information, and high-end assembly and manufacturing. It released *The Evaluation Index System of Hefei's Innovative Enterprises*,[5] which was the basis for appraising the innovation capabilities of such enterprises.

Creating Innovation Platforms and Implementing Key Projects

Science and technology innovation is a complex systematic process, requiring effective public service support. Under government direction, enterprises such as Xunfei, Jianghuai Automobile, Anhui Juyi Automatic Assembly Co., Ltd, and Hefei Forging Group closely cooperate with universities and research institutes. They have formed a series of industry–education–academy alliances in the fields of new energy power supply, electric cars, intelligent transportation, special assembly manufacturing, automatic assembly, and mechanical and electronic integration.

In 2007, Hefei set up an Innovation Public Service Centre to reduce the innovation cost for enterprises. The centre provides a one-stop service for participants to solve problems of equipment purchasing, finding and building partnerships, scientific research achievements, patented rights, government support, and seeking talent and expertise.

In 2009, based on the Innovation Public Service Centre, Hefei initiated three innovation bases for scientific research aggregation, incubation, and industrial upgrading. They are organised around six functions: to display achievements, successful cooperations, public service excellence, mediation between science and technology, purpose-built technology, and enterprise mentoring. In 2015, Hefei started to promote mass entrepreneurship, and the qualified incubators were able to get financial support from the local government.

The Achievements and Features of Building an Innovative City

The Achievements of Building an Innovative City

In January 2008, Hu Jintao, as secretary general of the CPC, visited the city, and said that 'Anhui has rich education resources and powerful science and technology capability. Anhui should achieve more from innovation.'[6] In response, Anhui Province set up the Hefei–Wuhu–Bengbu Testing

Figure 12.5: Chaohu Ecological Demonstration Zone

Areas of Independent Innovation, as a practical expression of Hefei as a pilot city. The role of the Testing Area is to eliminate obstacles that hinder innovation, and to explore an innovation-driven development mode to replace a factor-driven mode. On 17 October 2008, central government approved this proposal. Hefei took the lead in this new round of reform and experimentation. According to the blueprint issued by Hefei's science and technology conference held in 2013, the goal is for Hefei to become the national innovative city in 2015, and for the output value from high-tech industry to reach CNY1 trillion in 2017. Hefei is to become a global innovation centre by 2020.

Updating the Economic Structure and Changing the Development Mode

As noted, an upgraded secondary sector is to be the dominant element of the industrial structure (a ratio of 5.3:55.3:39.4). Hefei has become the new growth pole in the Yangtze River Delta and already per capita GDP has exceeded US$8,000.

This growth and upgrading goes alongside significant achievements in energy saving and environmental protection via 'light' and 'green' industrial development. In August 2011, Hefei started to construct the Chaohu Ecological Demonstration Zone – the most important project of Hefei's 'Great Lake City' strategy. In July 2014, Chaohu was approved in the first group of National Ecological Demonstration Zones.

Supporting the Strategy of Being an Industry-dominated City

Traditional industry and enterprises such as Hefei Forging, Heli Forklift Trucks, Meiling, and Rongshida have benefited from and been reinvigorated by the overall upgrading strategy. They now sit within the structure of energy-saving, environmental protection, and supportive government policy. The same overarching framework is the solid basis for the development of financial services, logistics, exhibition facilities and tourism, and creative cultural industries. It also encourages the development of SMEs in the relevant industrial chains and clusters.

Accumulating the Potential for Leapfrog Development

Since 2008, the number of authorised patents and patents of invention in Hefei has increased annually by 101.6 per cent and 36 per cent respectively. In 2014, expenditure of research and development in Hefei was 3.1 per cent of the total GDP, ranking it fifth among provincial capital cities. Patents on inventions were 12,929, ranking Hefei sixth among provincial capitals.

Increasing academic research is now translated into industry locally. Examples of leading technologies include voice synthesis, car and mechanical engineering, information home appliance manufacturing, radar manufacturing, traffic accident prevention, biological medicine, nanomaterials, and plant breeding. For example, iFlytek Co., Ltd has developed intelligent speech products and Jianghuai has developed Extended Range Electric Vehicles (E-REV).

Promoting the Aggregation of Innovation Resources

Hefei is becoming a locus for both national and international enterprises. Multinational high-tech enterprises and R&D organisations such as the Microsoft Technology Center, German Continental Tyres, and the Device Engineering Technology Research Center of National Biological Protection are settled there. National enterprises such as Haier, BOE, and Midea have joined them. This will lead to further inward migration of companies and talent.

Figure 12.6: Exhibition Hall of BOE Technology, Hefei

The Features of Building an Innovative City

Attracting External Investment and Developing Local Companies are Equal Priorities

The city especially encourages large-scale innovators which can also enhance local competence – together incubating high-tech enterprises. Attracting investment is seen as directly attracting talent.

Hefei Constructs Innovation Platforms to Nurture an Innovative Environment

Innovation platforms are a key mechanism in linking intellectual and research gains with industrial capability and financial vehicles. This requires a joint effort from government, universities, and enterprises to bring research to the market.

The Method of Fostering a Regional Innovation Ecology is to Apply the Experience from One Unit to a Whole Area

Anhui's regional innovation strategy has gone through three phases. In 2003, Anhui put forward the concept of 'Science City in Hefei'. This would only take up a few km^2. At the next stage, the Science and Technology Innovation Pilot City covered the whole geographical territory of Hefei. However, Hefei is not big and strong enough to drive the innovation activities of the whole Anhui Province on its own. It needs support from other cities in Anhui so, in a third stage, Wuhu and Bengbu joined Hefei in activating the science and technology resources throughout Anhui.

Hefei–Wuhu–Bengbu Innovation Comprehensive Reform Pilot Region is not only a geographical expansion for innovation, it also embodies a systematic network of resources, institutions, and organisations. More widely still, in September 2014, Hefei was positioned as the sub-centre of the Yangtze River Delta according to the Yangtze River

Figure 12.7: Institute of Advanced Technology, University of Science and Technology of China

Economic Belt Comprehensive Transportation Corridor Planning (2014–20). Thus, Hefei is now associated with Shanghai and the key provinces of Jiangsu and Zhejiang which make up the economic powerhouse of the lower Yangtze area.

In turn, Hefei and Anhui become a key stepping stone in the implementation of the One Belt and One Road Initiative as a link between the more open economy on the coast and the hinterland of China.

Endnotes

1   Hefei Overall Planning (2011–20), [EB/OL], http://www.hfsghj.gov.cn/ (accessed 26 April 2018).

2   Quoted from National Bureau of Statistics, *Hefei Statistical Yearbook*, China Statistics Press, 2014. Gross Domestic Product (GDP) means the value of total and final products and services produced in the economy of a country or region in a certain period. It is a key index that measures the economic development of a country or region.

3   'The best emerging business cities in China' (2012), *Fortune* (Chinese version), http://www.fortunechina. com/rankings/c/2012-09/14/content_116020.htm, (accessed 26 April 2018).

4   Science and Technology Innovation Enterprise Cultivation Plans, http://www.chinalawedu.com/ falvfagui/fg22598/222663.shtml 100 Enterprises Cultivation Project, http://www.9ask.cn/fagui/201203/88008_1.html

5   The Evaluation Index System of Hefei's Innovative Enterprises, https://wenku.baidu.com/ view/108c3a0d4a7302768e99397e.html

6   'Report of General Secretary of the CPC Hu Jintao's investigation in Anhui Province', *CCTV News*, 15 January 2008, http://cpc.people.com.cn/ GB/64093/66081/6776620.html (accessed 28 April 2018).

CONCLUSION

The present stage of China's urban development presents tremendous opportunities but only if a series of challenges are recognised and tackled. Urban policy has a well-defined and comprehensive perspective but this must also take account of the varied levels of development within the country, and also the specific historical and environmental evolution of each city.

In order to offer a well-rounded narrative of urban transformation, attention must be given to the spatial form of the city, its economic structure and the impact it has on its people's lives – its *liveability*. How people experience the city must now be the priority in considering the infrastructure and economy of place. For the city to be *liveable* citizens must experience the city as an environment in which material needs, cultural life, social and community relations, and ecological concerns are developed in balance and harmony.

This is a process of mobilising, organising, upgrading, and transforming each city according to its regional conditions and resource environment. At the same time, the day-to-day task of implementing, and operationalising, policy is set within a holistic vision for development with the following principles:

- To be people-centred and ecologically protective to make a habitable city.

- To co-develop industrialisation, agricultural modernisation, and informatisation for a well-balanced regional economy and environment.

At an early stage of our work we examined both domestic and international literature from which we constructed an evaluation model for upgrading capability and urban transformation. The model recognises that what is possible for each city depends first, but not only, on its endogenous qualities such as natural, historical, spatial, and economic features and also on a forward-looking and dynamic strategy provided by a national plan. Each city has its own place in the overall context for urban change.

The valuation model takes account of both elements and can continuously monitor the evolutionary trend of urban transformation and upgrading capability in Chinese mainland cities. The evaluation model highlights:

- 'People-centred' – well-being is the fundamental goal of development and people-centred development should be embodied in all aspects of urban transformation.

- 'Innovation-driven' – China's economy is in transition from a phase of rapid extensive growth to a stage of high-quality and more intensive development. Innovation is the primary driving force behind this crucial shift.

- 'Green ecology' – humanity and nature form a community. Sustainable development features increased productivity, higher living standards, and healthy ecosystems.

- 'Entrepreneur-friendly and habitable' – we should create good working and living environments for our people, so they will always have a strong sense of fulfilment, happiness, and security.

Due to the disequilibrium in China's economic and social development, there exist disparities in the urbanisation level between the cities in different regions. There are, therefore, different development models for urban upgrading and transformation. We selected six cities – Shanghai, Nanchang, Qingdao, Hangzhou, Chengdu, Hefei – as case studies to exemplify the key priorities.

These cities are located in different regions of China and have different resource endowments.

Although there is diversity in the content and direction of the transformation in the various cities, all aim to deliver **environmental protection, economic efficiency, and social justice** as the interwoven and fundamental goals of Chinese urbanisation, as follows:

- People-centred development is the starting point of urban transformation. People-centred transformation requires not only economic growth, but also social development, cultural progress, and environmental improvement.

- Urban change must be an integrated process, in which short- and long-term development sits within an overall perspective for space, infrastructure, industry, and social provision. This is the case whether it be single cities or city clusters.

- Urban transformation should match urban scale with the carrying capacity of resources and environment, match population concentration with industrial concentration, and adapt material production to cultural life.

- Urban transformation should pay attention to the optimisation of the whole urban system structure. Talent and resources are still too concentrated in the major urban cities, but with attention smaller cities can become attractive and convivial.

- A liveable, humanistic city is a fusion of its history, its lived present, and its future possibilities.

INDEX

Note: page numbers in italics refer to illustrations and figures; page numbers in bold refer to tables.

IMAGE CREDITS

Chapter 11

Chapter 12